HOW TO
Save
the World

AND RETIRE

HOW TO

Save the World

AND RETIRE

By GENE MONTERASTELLI

For information contact:
Brother Blue Publishing
PO Box 50395
Washington, DC 20091
BrotherBluePublishing.com

Cover and Interior Design: Pete Morelewicz

Manufactured in the United States of America

This is dedicated to all who try to follow God's will, regardless of where it leads them (and the people they love).

Contents

FOREWORD

Every one of us was created to live lives full of joy! I don't mean that in some cheap bumper sticker sentimental way. A joy which makes us lay awake at night, aching to live the lives we have created. I know this is possible because I have felt these moments. I have felt such fulfillment in life I was about burst with joy.

I am not going to lie and say every moment of my life is this way. But I want it to be. Every morning when I get out of bed I fight for abundant joy in my life. I believe you can do the same.

If it was only as easy as it sounds. Get up. Fight for joy. Find joy. Watch a little TV. Brush teeth. Go to bed. We both know that is not the case. Obstacles stand in the way of living joyfully everyday. Some of the obstacles are in the world and others are in our head's. No matter how large these obstacles seem, they are not insurmountable. Not only can we have this joy, but we were created to have this joy. I believe it is possible for you to live a life with passion and I believe this book will help you do that.

The book you hold in your hand is not full of secrets or tricks of the trade. Instead, it is a methodical process with two goals. The first half of the book will help you discover what your soul is longing for, your vocation (as you will see, I mean this in the broadest possible sense). It will help you craft a life in which you can find balance between family, work, and your faith life. You are not going to create a life that is necessarily easy and always fun, but a life you can live with passion. The second half of the book is geared to help you create a realistic financial plan to make this new life possible.

In my life I have found chasing dreams is as much fun (if not more fun) as having the dreams come true. My prayer is that as you work through this process is you will discover joy of living with passion. If there is anything I can do to help, don't hesitate to drop me a note.

¡Vaya con Dios!

Gene Monterastelli
gene@monterastelli.com

PART I

Your Life

Over the course of the last seven years I have crisscrossed the US and Canada. My work is a cross between being an itinerant preacher—that means I travel a lot—and a professional juggler—that means I get paid to throw up. In that time, I have met many youth ministers: ministers who have degrees and work full time, ministers who are right out of college trying to find their place in the world, ministers who are simply filling a void that needs to be filled because they know in their heart of hearts something needs to be done. I have been humbled many times by their work and dedication.

Youth ministers are really an odd lot. Not that being odd is a bad thing. If you called a youth minister "weird" they would thank you and wear it as a badge of honor. In general, they are lots of fun to be around, and I mean lots of fun. As part of their job description, they will publicly embarrass themselves at the drop of a hat in order to engage a teen. They love the work they do. Even more than that they love the young people they serve. Every youth minister I know sees their work as a blessing and a privilege.

With this great joy, there is also struggle. Many youth ministers are starving. I don't mean literally starving, though, with the salaries they are paid some are close to starving. I mean that they are starving *in their lives*. They work long strange hours. They don't have a lick of business sense. (I don't think I have ever seen *one* show up on time.) Most of them are working on a staff where they are on their own. They have supervisors who believe that there needs to be "something for the youth," but really have no idea what it is the youth minister does. Most have very small budgets, which do not include money for personal or professional development. For this, they get grief from their staff because their job is nothing more than "playing with the kids" and they always come in late. The fact that they were at the church until midnight the night before is lost. They lose touch with their peers because when their friends are having dinner on a Friday night, they are running a Jr. High dance. They are in a desert. Still they fight on, with passion and love.

Looking at their situation, I tried to figure out what I could do to help them, to feed them in some small way. What I really wanted to do was to become a trainer of youth ministers. But there are lots of trainers out there, and most of them are much more qualified than me. I sat back and tried to figure out what I could offer them that was unique. I realized maybe I could share my experience of balancing the work that I love with the pull of the material world. Maybe I could help them create and balance a life they could live with passion. In the end, that thought became this book.

Who This Book Is For

Does that mean that if you are not a youth minister this book isn't for you? No. They were the group that got me thinking. As I started to work on this book, I came to realize that most folks who are living lives out of passion didn't know how to find balance—how to manage their passions and their money. Whether your passion is for service, for art, or for family—think what it would be like to construct a life where you can pay your bills *and* see you child play basketball at 3:30 in the afternoon—you may well find yourself in the same situation.

If you are trying to figure out how to make a million dollars with no money down, this is not the book for you. If you are looking for a way to retire by the age of 40, this book is not for you. But, if you would like to live a life of passion, have balance in your life, and not lose sleep over the future, then you have found the right book. As you will see, this book is not really just about money. Money is just a tool. This is a book about filling your life with joy, abundant joy. If that is what you want, I invite you to continue reading.

Why am I qualified to write this book?

You might be thinking to yourself, *What makes this guy qualified to write this book? How did he come to some magic secret that no one else has?* The truth be told, I don't have magic secrets. What I have is life experience at making this work. I am a full-time minister. I have been able to take what I love—working with young people, traveling, and talking about myself (which I truly do love)—and make a living out of that, at the same time knowing that my financial future is secure.

For example, I love to travel. The only place I would rather be than on the road, is on the back of a horse. The prevailing wisdom about a desire to travel is: work hard, save your pennies, and you will be able to use your vacation days each year to do some traveling. Instead, I realized that if I found a job that paid for my travel, not only would my trips be paid for, but I wouldn't have to save up vacation days to take them. I took the time to identify what I love and then found a way to bring it in to my life. The entire first half of book is about coming to understand what truly brings you joy and finding way to bring those experiences into your life, not *just* in the work you do, but in many ways.

I might be qualified to talk about chasing dreams, but why would you take financial advice from a juggler? A good question! When I graduated from college I set it up so I wouldn't start my job as a computer programmer until September. This gave me the chance to see 23 states and three African countries. Chasing dreams from the start. Right after graduation I headed to my parents' house in Wyoming. One of the first days back my father asked me to come see him at his office. Growing up, the phrase "meet me at the office" usually meant I had done something wrong. At the age of 22, and still today, those words concerned me. To my surprise, I had not done anything wrong. I sat down across from my father. He said, "You are relatively moral," (thanks Dad) "you have a good education and are employable, but there is still one more thing as a parent I need to pass on to you." He handed me my first personal finance book THE WEALTHY BARBER by David Chilton. Then he said, "There will be a quiz." And I thought I was done with homework.

> Financial stability is not some magic formula, but instead a process of applying simple principles with discipline over the long term.

A week later we drove to a soccer tournament in another part of the state that we were both officiating and my siblings were playing. He drove and I sat next to him. He said, "Chapter 1, what is it about?" I explained everything I understood. Then he said, "Chapter 2, explain." This went on for the next two hours. In the end I realized that financial stability is not some magic formula, but instead a process of applying simple principles with discipline over the long term. It is also an issue of learning enough to understand how simple choices, made with discipline over time, will protect you in the future.

The financial information in this book is not earth shattering. To be honest, it is not really new, but you will see why this presentation is unique. This is not the only way to manage your life. This is based on my research and my experience. This process has worked for me, and I believe it can work for you.

Why This Book Is Different

There are lots of personal finance books on the market. A very good question would be: *Why is this book better?* Well, it's not, but it is different. Most personal finance books are only about money; this book is about *you*. Many of the financial principles you will find in other books you will find here. These are ideas that are very simple and time tested. The reason this book is different from the others is that before we talk about your finances, we will talk about your life. What you need, who you are, and want you want out of life for yourself and your family. Most other books will give you a list of tools, which are all necessary, but they don't address how those tools fit into *your* life. Other books assume that everyone has the same goals, and because of that everyone needs the same

> Change is not just our actions but our belief system.

information. That is simply not true. A life you live with passion is different from the next person's. Only when you define what that life looks like can you talk about how finances fit.

Financial tools are like a list of New Year's resolutions. We all know how resolutions work. First, we take an honest look at our lives and decide the things we would like to change. Then we make a list of steps we will take to make those changes. These are our resolutions. For the first two or three weeks of the year it works, but it doesn't last for long. Somehow we manage to slip right back into our old routine. It is not because we are weak, and it is not because we don't have will power. The reason we fail is we have made a list of actions that interrupt our lives. That can only last so long.

What we need to change is not just our actions but our belief system . Not our spiritual belief system but the ideas we hold about how life works. In the end, what other financial books are offering is a set of tools to fix your financial life. The tools are useful, and can make a difference, just like New Year's resolutions. The reason this book is different is because *first* you will get a stronger understanding of *why* you want to change your life and what your belief system is. When you have discovered *that,* the tools become much easier to use. Before we look at a real world example, let's spend a little more time with the term *belief system*.

In this context, when I use the term 'belief system' I am not talking about theological constructs, what you believe about God or the after life. I am not even talking about the difference between right and wrong. What I am talking about are the beliefs you hold which motivate your actions. I am talking about how you believe daily life works. In most cases these are beliefs you have not thought about in years, if you have ever thought about them consciously. Many times the beliefs are rooted in nothing more than, "that is the way it has always been." It is very important to understand your underlying belief system. It will be impossible to change your actions if you don't first change your belief system.

Let's take my friend Chris. Chris loves to eat. As a child growing up he was told he couldn't leave the kitchen table "until he cleared his plate." He had an Italian grandmother from the old country who had simple advice for every situation. Chris had a cold: "You need to eat." Chris had a fever: "You need to eat." Chris's girlfriend broke up with him: "You need to eat." Chris broke his leg: "You need to eat." Every family gathering was big meal. In Chris's belief system, the way the daily life works, food was generally equated with family, with good times, and with good health.

The problem, Chris is about 50 pounds over weight. His doctor has told him time and time again that he needs to lose weight or he'll be facing heart problems. Intellectually, Chris understood his diet was unhealthy. He'd read articles, he'd seen stories, and he had friends who'd had heart attacks much too young. Armed with this knowledge and encouragement from his doctor, he would do the diet and exercise thing. He would get on one diet, stick to it for a few weeks, and then slip. Really, how are you going to say "no" to your grandmother, who will take it personally if you don't eat a second helping of dessert?

After his next doctor visit, he would be motivated again to lose the weight and he'd jump on another diet. He would drop 30 pounds then somehow the weight would manage to creep back on. In some ways, the dramatic weight fluctuations Chris was going through were harder on his body than carrying too much weight. The reason Chris was on the weight rollercoaster was because he was trying to change his *actions*, not his *beliefs*. The thought of having heart trouble was not real to Chris. It was something that might happen, but more than likely would happen to someone else. Chris knew he needed to lose weight, but he was fighting a *belief system*—his entire history with food.

Then everything changed. His doctor was getting frustrated and was genuinely concerned about Chris's heath. The doctor said plainly, "Do you want to walk your daughter down the aisle at her wedding?" (She was 6 at the time.) "You need to lose 50 pounds and keep it off, or you are not going to be alive to do that." This was no longer some vague idea about needing to lose weight. It was real life.

Sometimes even that is not enough. We can have moments of revelation, but we quickly forget that revelation, and we slide (just like our resolutions). Chris decided he needed to do something to keep that revelation fresh in his mind—to change his belief system. He took his daughter to a wedding dress shop. He asked the manager if he could take a picture of his daughter in one of the full-size adult dresses.

Every day when Chris gets up he looks at that picture. Before every meal he looks at that picture. He placed one on the fridge at home and one on the snack fridge at work. He is reminded five or six times a day, not only that he needs to lose weight, but that he has a lot to live for. At a very core level he is changing his belief from "food is part of my family experience" "heart attacks happen to other people" to "I want to be around for a long time, therefore I need to control my food intake."

We make so many choices in our daily lives. Most of them we don't give a lot of thought to—the clothes we wear, the food we eat, the TV we watch. We base most of these choices on habit. These habits are formed by our belief system. On some level this is okay. If we took a great amount of time to make every decision in our lives, nothing would ever get done. Einstein owned seven identical sets of clothing, just so he didn't waste time thinking about his clothes. On the other hand, we need to understand that every choice we make *also* has a larger impact. For example, is the shirt I am about to purchase made in a sweatshop? We can't simply become mindless drones, acting only out of habit. We need to *understand* what we believe and *why* we believe that, and then ensure that we act accordingly.

THAT IS THE GOAL OF THIS BOOK It is to help you understand the things you want to live for, and to create a life that you can be passionate about. This book is about helping you choose to be the person you want to be, and live the life you want to live. To help identify the things you love, the experiences that feed you, and the things that make your soul soar. After that we will get to the money. We will begin to understand that money is important, but it is only a tool. We will find balance. How you choose a low-paying field like social work as a career and still send your kids to college. How you can fill your life with rich experiences, but not need endless riches. How you can save the world...and still be able to retire.

Why it is Important to Understand our Money

Most people want to start dealing with their money problems—right after they take care of that root canal. We feel money matters are very complicated. None of us likes feeling incompetent, especially about such an important subject. Most of us choose to deal with the things we don't understand by sticking our fingers in our ears and singing, "I can't hear you! I can't hear you! I can't hear you!" It can't be that way. We must deal with money, and do it now, for two reasons.

First, time is of the essence, as we will see in the second part of the book. Asking when to start thinking about money is like asking when the best time to plant a tree is—the best time is 20 years ago, the second best time is now. The longer you put this off, the harder it will be to get where you want to go. Most of us are not going to employ strategies that will make us rich quickly. We will use strategies which are less risky, but take more time. We must start now.

Second, every choice we make with our money is a statement about who we are. How we steward our resources expresses what we believe. The sooner we understand that, the sooner we can become the people we want to be. As Christians, we are called to steward every gift we have. The resources we have in our life are limited. We need to make sure that we are using them in a fashion that demonstrates who we are. Think of it like this, "What do my last ten purchases say about who I am?" With every action of our life we declare who we are, including how we use our money.

How to Use This Book

The temptation with every book is to get to the end, because the end is the best part. I am sure that temptation is especially true with this book. The reason you picked up this book, more than likely, is to understand how to manage your money. A quick look at the table of contents would show you we don't get to money until the second half of the book. The desire is to skip right to that section. Please don't do that. With this book, the end is not the best part—the process is the best part. Don't skip to the end. The second part of the book is nothing more than tools. If those tools are not rooted in the principles that are driving your life, they will not stick. You need to understand what you want your life to look like before you will be able to make disciplined choices. For me, the understanding of what life can look like is much more than just a question of money, it is the sum total of everything.

This book is not a bunch of tricks of the trade, or something you can jump around. Later, when you have developed a plan, it will be helpful to go back to particular sections to brush up, but not at first. It is a process that will take time. It will take reflection, prayer, and spending time in conversation with the loved ones in your life. Reading this book in one sitting might give you some ideas, but it will work best if you take time with each section before moving on. This book is about changing the way you think about your life. It is about understanding who you are called to be—a person whose life is filled with abundant joy. This is not something that will happen overnight. It will take time, but because it is a process that changes how you act in your daily life, it will have a much longer-term effect.

When you get into Parts III and IV of the book you will see there are a number of very specific activities that you will be asked to do. There will be a box that explains, step-by-step, how to do the activity. Some of the exercises build on previous exercises. One exercise in particular will have you review a number of other exercises for information. I strongly encourage you to do all of the exercises, but you'll also want to keep the exercises in one place. One suggestion I would make is to do *all* of the exercises in one notebook, starting a new page for each one. At the top of each page, write the name of the exercise on that page so when you look back it will be easy to find what you are looking for.

FOUNDATION

I sure you have noticed that I have used the phase *a life you can live with passion* a number of times. I believe that phrase sums up the thesis of this book. It is not a matter of finding one thing that brings you joy, but instead a totality of a number of aspects of your life. Naming all these aspects will help you see how each aspect plays off the other and then by keeping all these in balance, you create a life you can be passionate about. In understanding how this plays itself out in our lies I have found the term "vocation" very helpful. Don't get scared off by this word. Read on, you might find my working definition a little surprising.

Definition of Vocation

First let's take some time to understand what vocation is. Most often our understanding of vocation is related to the job we hold. In secular terms, "vocational training" is about the work we do. In more spiritual terms, the word "vocation" still lends itself to work, but most often we hear it in terms of working for the church in some formal fashion. I would like to speak about vocation in these terms but also to expand the definition even further. Vocation is not just about what we *do* but who we *are*. My vocation is not to be a storyteller. It is not to be a brother, a friend, a son, a teacher. My vocation is to be Gene. My vocation extends to every part of my life. A vocation will articulate itself very differently at 18 from how it will at 40. My vocation is not what I want to be when I grow up (if that ever happens). It is who I am right now *and* who I am called to become. How my vocation articulates itself will change based on the skills I have, the circumstances I am in, and the challenges I face. It is the sum total of my actions and beliefs. There is an incredible particularity and authenticity to our personal vocation — and that is given to change and develop over time as we grow. Throughout this book I will use the terms "vocation", "dreams", "God's will", and "what your soul longs for" interchangeably. To me they are all the same concept. They all describe a life you can live with passion. One or more of these terms may be useful to you, while others may have no meaning at all. If one description works for you and the others don't, simply substitute the image that works best.

But how do you know if you are living your vocation? This is a complicated question. If vocation is the sum of many different parts, and those parts are different for each person, it seems impossible to know. I would agree it is not something you know intellectually, but you can know it in your soul. If emotions are the language of the soul, then abundant joy is the way we know we're heading in the right direction. The feeling of joy is the signal that you are living your vocation. My vocation is what my soul longs to be every moment of my life.

Why It's Important to Understand Your Vocation

Just south of Washington DC is one of those mega-outlet malls. I have lost more than one Saturday inside it's walls. It is a monument to Western Civilization. I believe that two thousand years from now, the only four things that are going to be remembered about American culture are the Constitution, jazz music, barbecue, and outlet malls. I choose to believe history will bear at least three of those out as being positive.

Outlet malls are strange marketplaces. The basic philosophy is this: We have a bunch of stuff that is so hideous that we can't sell it in our regular stores. If we put all the ugly stuff together and charge very little money for it then people will buy it. The odd thing is — it works! I'm not sure if this is because we can't say no to a bargain "Look! These pants only cost six dollars!" "Yeah, but they have a forty-two inch waist and are plaid." "I know, but they are only six dollars!"— or if it's just that when everything is ugly, it all looks less ugly by comparison.

> If emotions are the language of the soul, then abundant joy is the way we know we're heading in the right direction. The feeling of joy is the signal that you are living your vocation. My vocation is what my soul longs to be every moment of my life.

Personally, I enjoy shopping at an outlet mall. I enter with a plan. I am looking for a pair of green corduroy pants and I will not pay more than nine dollars for them. I am on a mission. I hop from store to store with only one goal in mind. I only enter stores that might meet my needs, and if they don't have exactly what I'm looking for, I move on. The only interruption to my laser—like focus is a stop at Orange Julius. It is great fun, for I am on the hunt. In the same vein, I can think of no worse experience than wandering into an outlet mall with no plan. The next thing you know, it is five hours later. You have managed to spend close to a hundred dollars on stuff that you will never wear, and you have no idea where you parked. In an oversimplified and probably ridiculous analogy, our direction in life is very similar to walking into the outlet mall.

If we know what we want, we are more likely to get it. It is possible to wander aimlessly and find a real gem. As someone's grandfather once said, "From time to time, even a blind squirrel finds a nut." None of my grandparents said anything nearly that corny. But more than likely, without a plan, we just wander. We'll end up with the size 42 plaid pants and a really big pretzel. Knowing what a life you can live with passion looks like will make it a whole lot easier to reach for your soul's desires.

If we know what we want, we eliminate a large amount of stress in our lives.

If we know what we want, we are more likely to get it.

Most stress comes from feeling a lack of control. We are stressed because we don't have enough money, we don't feel safe, or we don't know what we want in life. These fears and anxieties stem from feeling like we are at the mercy of fate. When we feel that we are in control, even if we are a long distance from our goal, we are much more at peace. Recently I sat down with a couple. As we were working through their finances, we wrote on a sheet of paper every single debt and outstanding bill, what the minimum payment was, and the interest rate of each. Not including their home, the total was over twenty-five thousand dollars which is not uncommon for an American family. The wife almost started to cry. Then in fifteen minutes we worked out a plan, a plan that would require discipline and sacrifice, which would have them out of debt in twenty-one months. Twenty-one months is a long time to tighten the belts, but the anxiety was now gone. It was a big task, but now the task was clear. A plan of attack had been formulated in small, manageable steps. What was once an unclear very large problem had become an understandable large problem with a solution. The problem was no smaller fifteen minutes later, but they were back in control.

If we know what we want, if we have a purpose in life, it improves our sense of identity and our ability to believe in ourselves. One of the biggest hurdles to feeling like we are in control, is thinking that we cannot gain control. It is a downward spiral. We don't have control, so we lose self-esteem. As we lose self-esteem, we feel that we have less control. It goes on an on. By having a goal to work toward, we are now able to say about ourselves: "This is where I am heading." By simply having a purpose, we are able to give our life value because we can name what we are pursuing, in turn improving our self-esteem.

If we know what we want, it simplifies our lives. It puts us on the path to where we want to go and helps us identify the places we don't. When we know what we want, it is easier to approach every action we take and ask the question, "Is this part of who I want to be?" If the answer is "no" then we don't do it and move on.

Joy vs. Happiness

Joy does not equal happiness. Happiness is a fleeting moment. It can come and go very quickly. It is not necessarily something that lasts. It is on the surface. Someone unexpectedly brings you an ice cream cone. This will bring you a moment of happiness, but is not something that moves your soul. Joy is much deeper. Joy has to do with the orientation of your life. Joy is found at the depths of who you are. It is possible to be unhappy in the moment, but still be filled with joy at your depth. Picture the ocean. From moment to moment, the surface of the ocean can be calm or it can be a raging storm, but down in the deep, it is always the same. There have been many times in my life when I have been unhappy (doing the taxes for the ministry I help run), but in my soul I have joy, because I am doing work that truly lights me up.

In this case: SURFACE = UNHAPPY   DEPTH = JOY

But this does not mean that the surface doesn't affect the depth. If a storm rages for days, it will eventually affect the depths of the ocean; in the same way, the events on the surface of our lives can affect our depths (read "soul"). For example, you might be working for a boss who belittles you, takes credit for your work, and constantly comes in at the last minute telling you that you need to stay late. These are inconveniences to a job you love, every job has them. If these things happen once or twice, they can be hurtful and frustrating, but it would not affect your long-term feeling about your job. If they happen consistently over a long period of time, it will start to affect your depth. At a certain point the pain of being at work becomes so great you can no longer do your work well, you are taking your frustrations home, and it becomes impossible to carry on. The surface has sucked your joy away.

It is important to have happiness in our lives, but joy is much more permanent. When we are living the lives our soul longs for we will have many more moments of happiness, but much more importantly at our core we will be filled with joy. The hallmark of a life you live with passion is an abundance of joy. When you act with passion, joy follows.

Our goals here are: (1) to name what brings you joy, leading you to understand your vocation, leading you to craft a life you can live with passion and (2) to create a financial situation where you have the stability to pursue that joy, even through change.

Money Is Nothing More Than a Tool

Money is such a frightening subject to talk about. We are taught from a very early age that it is not proper conversation to talk about politics, religion, sex, or money. Often (whether we mean to or not) we use money as a scorecard. We use it to define our value. I am not going to say money is not important—it is—but I hope to help you put money in perspective. Money is a tool, nothing more, nothing less. Money was created so we wouldn't have to use the phrase "do you have change for a chicken?" when we go shopping. (Because before there was money we bartered for everything. Get it? Change for a chicken, like the chicken is money? Nevermind.)

Money, like all tools, has no morality. Money is not good or bad. Money is a tool. Take a hammer for example. A hammer has no morality. It is not good or bad. The hammer is not what is important. What is important is how I use the hammer. I could choose build a house with the hammer or I could choose to break my brother's finger with the hammer. One is a desired outcome; the other is not. (Building the house is the desired outcome.) Money is no different. What is important is how we use it.

Using the lens of "tool" to understand money will begin to free us up from being scared of money. Money can be a very intimidating subject. Before we are done, it will be less so. Money is an important tool, but money has no importance in and of itself.

How Money Fits into a Life Lived with Passion

Money is not the be all and end all of our existence. It does not give us worth. It does not give us comfort. It can't give us love. At the same time, we can't simply ignore money either. We live in the world. We need a place to live. We need to eat. Health insurance is more than just a good idea. Where does money fit in? Money is not essential to life, but it is important. The best way I can describe the difference between *essential* and *important* is with a story.

A few years ago I watched one of my best friends bury her father. Allen died suddenly of a heart attack at the age of 54. The work Allen had given his life to was important. He trained military officers to deal with hijackers. He trained special ops to manage hostage crisis. He was called in as part of a very small group of professionals from all over the US, to help the workers at Ground Zero of the World Trade Center deal with the emotional fallout of their work. Allen was self-employed and had to work long hours to provide for his family. The work he did was important and he was very skilled at it..

Days before Allen died he had the first in a series of heart attacks. After surgery he was resting comfortably in the hospital with his three daughters and his wife. He turned to his daughters and said, "You know, I would really loved to have taken you girls camping." The three of them looked at him, dumbfounded. One of them said, "But, Daddy, we are three of the girliest girls ever. We wouldn't have liked camping." Allen paused and replied, "I would have liked to find out."

Allen has spent his whole life doing wonderful work. He loved his work. His family believed in his work. The work he did provided for the family, but as Allen was looking death square in the eye (a battle he lost two days later) he and his family were given a moment of perspective. They all understood his work was important, but in that moment they re-realized that time together as a family was more than important. It was essential.

Money is very important. We live in a material world. It is the basis for most of our commerce. Even though money is important, ask Allen's daughters, hey can tell you the difference between *important* and *essential*.

In this book I hope to help you understand what is important and what is essential in your life, and how those things work in concert with each other. No where in this text will you find a list of what's important and what's essential. That is different for each of us because we each are a unique creation, with a unique vocation. Even in situations where parts of our vocations are similar, they will express themselves differently in each life. Instead, what you will find is a process that will help you determine which is which. You will have to work hard to keep the mundane from getting in the way of the important, but you have to work just as hard to keep the important from hurting your ability to tend to the essential.

Rich vs. Poor

Most of us don't lay awake at night dreaming of having millions of dollars. From time to time as we are flipping around the dial and we see some TV program showing off the insides of a movie star's house. We think it would be nice to live like that. And every time there is a big hit in the lottery we ask our friends, "What is the first thing you would do if you won a hundred million dollars?" They are fun fantasies to have, but most of us are content to know that we will never be driving Bentleys or owning private jets. Even with this realistic view, we do feel like it would be nice to have more money. In her book THE SOUL OF MONEY, Lynne Twist shares a very interesting perspective on wealth and poverty. Lynne Twist has worked with the Hunger Project for more than 25 years to eliminate hunger in the world. Because she works as a fundraiser, she works with people who are very wealthy. Because she works to fight hunger she also works with some of the poorest people in the world. She refers to those we would call

> The goal is not resource richness, but to create and embrace the richness of your own life.

rich and poor as "resource rich" and "resource poor." In story after story, she recounts the *poverty of the soul* (Mother Teresa's term) of the resource rich, and the rich lives of the resource poor. That is not to say there is not happiness amongst the resource rich, or being resource poor is the key to happiness, but instead that resources are not the only factor, nor the most significant one, in living a rich life. I don't make a lot of money in the work that I do, but I have a very rich life. The key is to understand the goal is not resource richness, but to create and embrace the richness of your own life.

PART II

The Call

CHOOSING TO FOLLOW YOUR SOUL

"It is easier to be the happiest person in the world than it is to be the richest."
Bill Walton

Dreaming of a better life

There are few things that I hold in more reverence than someone's dreams. In my mind, dreams are what the soul is longing for. It is a tricky matter dealing with dreams and, many times, we don't deal with dreams very well. Dreams often occupy one of two extremes in our lives. Some dreams are treated so grand we won't even speak them out loud. They are something we really long to do, but we fear chasing them because they are unattainable, or we don't speak them aloud because we fear others will think us foolish. The other extreme is to treat dreams as nothing more than filler. As we hang out with friends, we talk about the restaurant that we will open together one day. Everyone knows it is never going to happen. We are just filling time in a fantasy land. There is a balance that needs to be struck. The task you are undertaking is serious. The questions you are asking are sacred, but they should not only be asked in hushed tones. Our vocation is a tricky topic that we don't feel comfortable talking about. The more time you spend with the topic, the more comfortable you will become. As you think about your dreams and give them a real face, your fears will slowly melt away. You will find when you start asking these questions the journey will become much more important than the answer. If you are going to change your life for the better, you will need to live your dreams out loud.

As children we were given license to indulge the dreams we had. We were encouraged to use our imaginations and play pretend. Imaginary friends were treated by the family as full-blooded family members. One moment we were scaling a castle in the back yard, and the next were hacking our way through the jungle fighting ants that were six feet tall. One day all of this dreaming stopped, and we became adults. There was no right of passage that we made into adulthood. Somehow, one day, we were just adults. And somehow, one day, we became *responsible*. We are now supposed to be serious and mature. As adults it is frowned upon to use imagination. Pondering exotic dreams is childish, and childish is not tolerable for respectable adults. I wish I knew why this was. We just know we should keep our heads down, work hard, and not rock the boat. We love dreamers who come up with art and innovation, but that is done by special people. Only artists make great art, for the rest of us art is just a hobby. It is fine to show our work to the immediate family, but we should not dream that our work has any value or that anyone would really care to see it. Those who come up with great inventions are special people. They are blessed by the heavens to be geniuses. Those are the people who are allowed to dream. Those are the people who are allowed to think big thoughts. Those are the geniuses who are granted the right to think big thoughts. But not us. We are...well...adults. No, we are *responsible* adults.

Hog wash!

Right now, if you know it or not, there are giant dreams hiding in your soul. This is what your soul is longing for. This is your calling. There is no question. They are in there. And it is not that there is one dream inside you, but lots of them. There are dreams about your family, your relationships, the work you do, and how you can provide for yourself and your loved ones. You are still a dreamer, even if you are out of practice. The dreams that you have inside you are important. The dreams that are inside of you, is your soul calling out for a fuller richer life. Those dreams are a window into your vocation. It is time once again to be a dreamer. You have been blessed by the heavens with genius, the genius to be yourself to the richest fullest extremes. In order to do this, you will have to listen to your dreams, and in turn listen to you soul. It is time to be brave. It is time to be a dreamer once again. It is time to listen to your soul to create a rich life you can live with passion.

Where You Are Right Now

Right now I have no idea where you are in your life. I have a feeling that if you picked up this book it is because you want a better life. Either you are not living the life you want, or you feel that you have no control when it comes to your finances (or both). You are not alone. With the two statements I have just made, I would contend that there are more people who are in the same boat as you than you would imagine. For some reason, we feel like we should always know what we are doing and know where we are going. We leave so little room in our culture for doubt. Some unknown force is requiring definitive action. Let go of those feelings. You are allowed to not know exactly what you want. As long as you recognize that you are unsatisfied with your life and are actively trying to make it better, you are in the right place. In my mind, because you are asking the questions, you are in a better place than those who think they know what they are doing. We are unfinished, and always will be in our lifetime. The best we can hope for is to be moving in the right direction. There are times in our lives when we won't be heading in the right direction, but if we keep questioning which path we are on, we will figure it out.

Wherever you are in your life right now is okay. I know it is not where you want to be, but the fact of the matter it is where you are. What you need to be willing to do is acknowledge honestly what your life looks like in every aspect. Don't kill yourself over the mistakes you have made, but realize you have made them. The same is true with the parts of your life that you love. Look at those parts honestly as well. Be proud of what you have, but not arrogant. With a clear understanding of where you are, this becomes the jumping off point to creating the life you dream about.

Fear and Loathing

My father has always said, "A little fear is good." I would agree. A little fear (of my father) was a great motivator growing up to keep my nose clean. I don't want you to completely lose your anxiety, but too much anxiety is debilitating. If we worry too much, we become consumed by it and are paralyzed. A little fear, on the other hand, will serve as a great motivator. As we move through this experience, let your fear motivate rather than debilitate.

Just because you have picked up this book doesn't mean you are out of the woods. In the time it takes you to read this book, your life is not going to magi-cally change. You will have to ask yourself a number of hard questions, and what's more difficult, you will need to be honest with yourself. If you go through this process honestly, you will shine a light on a number of parts of your life that you are dissatisfied with (otherwise, why would you be reading this?). I can't stress enough how hard this might be, to look at who you are honestly, but you have to do it. As you look at the mistakes you have made in your past, you will feel regret. It is okay to look at those choices with regret. You may feel like you have failed. Regret can be a very helpful emotion. It is a way to recognize that you would like to have acted differently. When we regret a choice, we can learn from the mistake and move on. What you need to watch out for is feelings of guilt. Guilt is not a helpful emotion. Guilt is an emotion that doesn't center on the poor choice, but on the idea you are a bad person. Guilt is debilitating and destructive. Guilt will not serve you. I am not saying that you shouldn't own up for the choices you made in the past. You must take responsibility, but with regret you deal with the consequences. With guilt you never move past the poor choice.

For a few moments put this book down. Think about your life. Think about your family. Think about your work, your health, your money. What parts of your life look the way you want them to look? Name the parts of your life that you don't like in their current state, and which parts you feel like you have lost control over. Don't linger too long on this, or be consumed by negative emotions. Just know what the starting point is.

Paralysis of Choice

A second challenge you will face is the fact that you will have to make choices about your life. Choices can be scary. As dissatisfying as it is to not have the life you want, it can be easier to complain about it than to do something constructive. Sometimes we feel like it is better to deal with the problems we know, than open the Pandora's Box of problems that are unknown. I may be suffering now, but I know this suffering. I can manage this suffering. Choosing something new could be wonderful or it could be much worse that it is right now. Choices can cause us to lock up and have paralysis.

I was having dinner with a group of my friends and Mary was talking about the next step in her career. In order to make what she thought was the next logical move, she would have to change jobs, probably change locations, and take on much more responsibility. Another friend at the table, who is connected nationally in Mary's field, was excited by Mary's dream. He started listing off all the jobs in the region that were open that she could apply for right now. You could see Mary's mind come to a grinding halt. It was nice to think what the next step was, but, to look at and understand the reality of making that change was too much for her. It was no longer a nice idea of some distant future, or a story to tell when she was feeling unsatisfied in the position she was in. It was reality. It was not only something she could have, but something she might fail at. Chasing dreams can be something you can pay lots of lip service to, or it can be an action that at times will be a bit scary.

Sacrifice

In order to change your life you will need to make sacrifices. Simply naming what you want your life to look like is not going to make it happen. There are many benefits to naming where you would like to go, but those benefits are short-lived if you don't do anything about those dreams. I am going to assume that in order to get onto the right track financially, you will have to make sacrifices in the long term. For most Americans, when they are getting their financial lives in order, they are not only trying to make right choices in the future, but they are correcting mistakes of the past. In order to do this you will need to make sacrifices. You will need to make other sacrifices as well. You might have to sacrifice time to get a missing piece of education in order to chase your dream. More than likely, as you name what you want in your life, you will realize that your dream life goes against the grain of the culture at large. It might require you to live in a smaller house, drive a used car, or to do a job that you love—but the world thinks is silly. There is a great deal of pressure in our society to be like everybody else, to value the same things. It is hard to go against the grain in our beliefs, in our work, and in our lifestyle choices. All of us struggle with wanting to fit in. You will have to sacrifice that feeling of comfort that comes with fitting in. I am not saying that if you follow your dreams you will become a leper, but you will end up living the value system that fits your life, not others. As you follow your dream, you may realize that you will need to change jobs. You will have to sacrifice the job you don't like. That may not seem difficult but you might be seen as a quitter. You might feel like you are letting down those you work with. The new guy won't know what is going on and it will make it harder for your old co-workers. That is sacrifice.

I am not saying this to scare you off or to discourage you from making choices in your life. I want you to have an extraordinary life, but you don't *just* have an extraordinary life. It is something that must be created and it is something that takes work. At times the work will be hard, and the future might seem uncertain, but I can think of no more worthwhile journey. I think one of the main reasons that we hold back our pursuit of dreams is the fear that we will make the wrong choice and are not going to get the time back. We feel if we make the sacrifice and it's wrong we have wasted our lives.

I have read a number of studies and interviews done with people who have been diagnosed with terminal illnesses. Time after time they talk about how liberating it is to know that they were going to die. They no longer feel tied up by some unknown future. They are liberated to live the life they truly want. By understanding that they had a limited time to live, they knew they couldn't waste a minute of it. They were willing to sacrifice, because they understood that regardless of the choice they made, they were going to die soon. In their minds it was better to die rying to do what they wanted instead of dying living the safe life they had. We, on the other hand, have uncertain futures. We clutch the minutes we have tightly to our chest in hopes not to waste them, but in the end that is all we are doing. In reality, we too have a terminal illness. It is called life. We are all going to die. Most of us simply don't know when that is going to be.

Why It's Okay to Be Selfish

You might be thinking, *Isn't this all a little selfish to be thinking just about what I want?* Being selfish is okay. It really is. I am not talking about the way a 2-year-old is selfish, hoarding everything in sight because in their mind they are the center of the universe, or as my friends in Spain say, "What do you think you are, the belly button of the Earth?" What I am saying is you need to be selfish in the sense that every choice you make is the choice that you really want to make. I try to be selfish in every choice I make. That doesn't necessary mean every choice I make is self-serving. I think it is a selfish choice to go and spend time helping

> To be selfish is to make every choice the choice that you really want to make.

out at a soup kitchen. It is a selfish choice because I want to help, because I see those I am able to serve as the Body of Christ that I am living in communion with. It is selfish because I am choosing who I want myself to be. In this sense, every choice you make should be selfish, a choice you are making to define yourself. You should not make any choice because you have to. I literally mean no choice. As a parent, when your child is sick in the middle of the night, you don't get up and comfort them because you have to. You do it because you love your child. You have made a selfish choice because you were choosing who you wanted to be, a loving parent.

This kind of selfishness should take hold in every aspect of life. The choices you make about how you spend your money, how spend your time, and how you spend your talent. It is in these choices that you define who you are. It is only when you take responsibility for these choices, and the consequences for these choices, that you will start to craft your life and understand what your vocation is.

THE NATURE OF VOCATION

Discerning God's will in our life is a tricky business. To start I would like to offer a story that I am sure you have heard before:

ONCE UPON A TIME THERE WAS A TREMENDOUS STORM WHICH WAS CAUSING MASSIVE FLOODING. IT WAS DECIDED FOR THEIR OWN SAFETY THAT ALL OF THE

RESIDENTS OF A SMALL TOWN NEEDED TO BE EVACUATED. WHEN THE SHERIFF APPEARED AT ONE PARTICULAR DOOR TO ASK THE RESIDENT TO LEAVE, HE RECEIVED SOME RESISTANCE. THE MAN WHO LIVED THERE SAID, "I AM NOT LEAVING. GOD WILL SAVE ME!" THE RAIN CONTINUED FOR SEVEN MORE DAYS AND THE SHERIFF RETURNED TO THE HOUSE. THIS TIME HE RETURNED IN A SMALL BOAT BECAUSE THE LAND HAD FLOODED. WHEN HE ARRIVED AT THE MAN'S HOUSE HE BEGGED HIM TO EVACUATE. ONCE AGAIN THE MAN SAID, "I AM NOT LEAVING. GOD WILL SAVE ME!" THE RAINS CONTINUED FOR SEVEN MORE DAYS. AGAIN, THE SHERIFF RETURNED TO THE MAN'S HOUSE, BUT THIS TIME THE FLOODING WAS SO HIGH HE CAME IN A HELICOPTER. WHEN HE GOT TO THE HOUSE HE FOUND THE MAN SITTING ON HIS ROOF BECAUSE THE HOUSE WAS UNDERWATER. THE SHERIFF BEGGED HIM TO LEAVE FOR HIS OWN SAFETY, BUT AGAIN THE MAN SAID, "I WILL NOT LEAVE. GOD WILL SAVE ME!" THE RAIN CONTINUED FOR SEVERAL MORE DAYS AND THE MAN DROWNED. WHEN THE MAN GOT TO HEAVEN, TO SAY THE LEAST, HE WAS A LITTLE FIRED UP. HE WALKED UP TO GOD AND SAID, "HOW COULD YOU LET ME DROWN IN THAT STORM? WHY DIDN'T YOU SAVE ME? I PUT ALL MY FAITH IN YOU." GOD REPLIED, "WHAT DO YOU MEAN NOT SAVE YOU? I SENT THE SHERIFF TO SAVE YOU THREE TIMES."

For most of us, the skies will not part with trumpeting angels. There will not be a command, "You are to do x with your life." If only it were that simple. For some people it might be that simple. There are people who, for as far back as they can remember, have known what their soul wants. Don't feel inadequate if you are not in that situation. Success is in the life you live, not in comparison to others. But alas, that is not the experience most of us are going to have. How do we start? By listening to our soul.

Success is in the life you live, not in comparison to others.

The call of our soul unfolds in our lives. It will not be a path that lays out before you. We will not be able to see past the horizon or what is on the other side of the next hill. Many times we won't see the end of the path or even the path ahead, but only the step in front of us. I know many times in my life I have thought I have seen the path before me, but it was nothing more than a mirage. But it was not the mirage of the oasis that Daffy Duck sees in the desert only to be throwing sand into his mouth instead of the water he thinks is there. For me, the mirage was simply an incomplete vision. By moving towards the mirage, I was able to move towards something I could not see. The only time I have been able to truly see the path is with hindsight. It is only in the past that I can connect the dots of my life to see how one experience leads to the next. For most of us it will unfold slowly before us as we keep trying to press forward.

In the Galleria de l'Accademia in Florence, there is a hallway that leads to the large hall which houses Michelangelo's David. The hallway is lined with ten of Michelangelo's slaves. Each of the sculptures is a large block of rock; they are in varying states of completion. Even within each sculpture there are degrees of completion. The right leg might be completely formed while the upper arm is still rough and just starting to take shape. As I was looking at the statues I was listening to the audiotape guide of the museum. The narrator explained how Michelangelo believed each piece of rock had a sculpture inside of it. It was not his job as sculptor to decide what the rock should be sculpted into, but instead to discover what was inside the rock and pull it out. The reason one part of the body would be complete and smooth while another was still very rough was because the sculptor was still trying to find what was calling out to be created. Our lives are the same. As time passes we sometimes come to a better understanding of one part of our lives, our relationships with our family for instance, while gaining no insight in another, perhaps the work we are to do. We will not see the whole vision. We will not be done at once. Each step down the path is one more chip of rock as we sculpt our lives.

In the chapters that follow, there will be a number of exercises for you to do. The exercises are designed to help you look at the block of rock at this time in your life, giving you a new way to look at your life and to listen to your soul. The process we will use is not science, it is not a formula. It is nothing like a COSMO quiz, where you answer questions, get their point value, add them up, and know your future. This process is art. It requires creativity. It requires self-examination. Art is not an answer to a question. Art is a process and the result of the process is an experience, a story. That is what you are going to craft, a story—the narrative of your life.

The Seven-Year Overnight Success

One of my guilty pleasures is to read ENTERTAINMENT WEEKLY. I love movies and am fascinated by pop culture, but I know the time I spend reading it will not make me a better person. I read it because it is fun. I have always enjoyed the interviews with the new flavor of the month. Some hot new band that in the next few months mainstream radio is going to play to death. It is generally a time in an artist's or band's career in which their life is just starting to change in radical ways. One day they are playing dive bars, the next stadiums. Inevitably they are asked the question, "What does it feel like to be an overnight success?" Just as inevitably the artist is shocked by the question, "What do you mean overnight success? We have been a band for over seven years. The success we have has taken seven years." For the outsider it is hard to see those years of work because they happened in obscurity. From the outside it looks like overnight.

Following our vocation is often no different. Many times it will take years and years to come to fruition. That is not to say it is not worth the time and effort, but it is important to note it that is a journey. For example, in Part IV of the book when we talk about finance, the second step is to eliminate debt. Naming that we want to eliminate debt takes only a moment, but the process could take as long as two or three years. More than likely, your story will be a seven-year overnight success story.

Energy to Act

Try driving I-80 across the state of Nebraska. You can drive for hours and hours and feel like you are getting nowhere because there is little change in the scenery. I can remember driving home from college. I was sick, loopy from the medication I was on, and wanted nothing more than to be out of the car and home. My travel companion and I were making the best time we could (legally). Still, it was taking forever. I thought Nebraska was never going to end. We stopped for the night in western Nebraska, just five hours short of my home in Wyoming. As we unloaded the car for the night I heard it: the simple call of a bird. I can't say it was a beautiful song, but it was a sound I knew by heart. It was the sound track of my youth, the song of the Western Meadowlark. Even though the landscape hadn't changed, there was a hint that I was close.

Passion is the element of our soul that turns labor from work into joy.

Often when we act or following a plan, we feel like we are treading water. Getting no were. I have yet to experience something that my soul has called for that was easy. Many times something rang so deeply in my soul and I ached to do it. Still, it was not easy. Following a dream is like a many-step journey. Many times with journeys we may be moving forward, but not know it. The first time I looked out over the Grand Canyon, I was camping about an hour from the rim. I hiked along the path. I wasn't wearing a watch so I had no idea how long I had been on the trail, or how much further I had to go. For the most part the trail looked the same, dirt and rocks below my feet and trees on both sides. Then in an instant the trees broke and the whole canyon appeared, as if this massive canyon could simply hide around a corner.

When we chase dreams, there will be stretches when we will feel like we are not getting any closer. We feel as if we are treading water, the seven years before our overnight success. How do we sustain? How do we keep moving? First, it is a matter of will. You have to keep choosing to move forward. But it has to be more. Will is an intellectual act. It is a choice to do something. Even with the strongest of discipline and intellectual understanding, there has to be more to sustain us. That "more" is passion. Passion is the element of our soul that turns labor from work into joy. This is how you will know if your soul is longing for something, if there is passion present. Passion will become your storehouse of energy. It will be what keeps you going. Long after the initial rush of doing something new wears off, there will be passion. A slow-burning energy deep in the soul. Think back to our example of Chris and the weight he wanted to lose. Willpower had never been enough. It was only when he identified passion that he could follow through on his commitment to change his life. Passion is what gives us strength to carry on in the hard times. There will be times in which we think we are chasing our soul's desire and we will discover that there is no passion. It might have been an experience we have enjoyed, that energized part of our personality, but not our whole soul. We simply must learn from the experience. Take a deep breath and try again. Our first quest is to name your passion so that when you feel you can't carry on, you will be able to remind yourself what you are journeying toward. This will give you the strength to go forward.

Questions, Not Answers

I have found in my own life that no matter what process I followed, no matter how faithful I was in taking time to pray and listen to my soul, I did not get answers. Instead I got questions. In many ways, these questions have been much more instructive than answers. When I have asked questions and have gotten answers (in anything), my search ended. If the answer was satisfying enough, I was done, but so was my growth with the question I first posed. When I have received a question back it has caused me to continue my journey. A question I have asked for many years now is, "How am I to act in the world?" One oversimplified theological answer is to follow the Ten Commandments. If that was the answer I accepted, I would stop challenging my actions and simply follow those ten rules and prohibitions. Thankfully that is not the answer that I have heard in prayer. At one point in my life the answer I received was another question, "What does it mean to act with unconditional love?" After spending time trying to wrap my little mind around what unconditional love was, it gave me a way to frame every choice I made. I would enter a challenge and I would ask myself, "How would I act with unconditional love in this situation?" When I was attentive enough to ask the question it helped me in all my actions. By not having a pat answer of how to act (read "directive"), I was given a chance to choose how I wanted to create myself in the situation.

Don't be deterred if in the process ahead you find more questions than answers. It is important to keep trying to find your way. As you move forward, be open. Our lives can be magical journeys even if we don't travel great distances. The reason we love stories is that we want to see what is next. We might think we know but we have to turn the page to find out. Sometimes we are happy because it turns out how we hoped. Other times we are pleasantly surprised by the ending. The stories of our lives should be no different. As we seek out the answer to the question *What is my soul longing for?* we are not necessarily going to get answers. What we know we will get is the next chapter.

Making Change

Choosing to follow the longing of your soul is not a choice that you make once, it is living a life you are passionate about. It is in the choices you make over and over again, because you are choosing who you want to be. We make choices everyday, though we don't think about it. Everyday we choose what job we will do. The only time it may feel like a choice is when we make a change, like when we choose to work somewhere else, but in reality we are choosing our job every day. Nothing is forcing you to go into work. You choose to do it. It may not feel like a choice, because we run on autopilot, but we are choosing. No one can tell you what choices to make. What is important, in my mind, is the fact that we are choosing. We are not doing what we did the day before simply out of habit, but by thought and desire.

Oftentimes, it takes us quite a while to realize that our soul is discontent. It is only after a long period of time that we realize that there needs to be a major change in our lives. These changes can be hard. When things are good, not great, we *talk* about change. But it's when things are bad we actually make changes. In his book CALLINGS: FINDING AND FOLLOWING AN AUTHENTIC LIFE, Gregg Levoy points out that sometimes, when the fear of making a change is overtaken by the pain of not making a change, only then are we capable of making a change. It is like an addict who has to hit rock bottom before he or she will accept the need for recovery.

In order to make a change you have to be committed to the change. You may start to understand what your soul is longing for but find that you are not capable to act. When you hear the voice of resistance to, pay attention to it. Hear that voice out. Hear the resistance out loud. Maybe it is well-founded, telling you to wait, or it may be a phantom of fear posing as the soul telling you not to act.

Shut Up and Listen! Don't Think too Much

For some reason one of the things we don't do well, particularly in American culture, is handle silence. Our lives are filled with noise and activity. When we get up in the morning, we turn on the radio as we get ready for the day. As we eat dinner we have the TV on. When we are in the car the radio is on. Recently, I had gotten to the point in my life where I couldn't fall asleep without the TV or radio on. The silence was too much. I am convinced part of the reason that many people live in major cities is because the noise drowns out the silence. Silence makes us uncomfortable. One of the ways I know I have made a true friend is when I am able to sit with them, say nothing, not feel compelled to fill the void, and not feel like I have to apologize for the silence.

In reality there is no such thing as silence. There is just lack of noise. We all know that even when we are quiet there is an internal dialogue that is constantly going. Images, words, and memories just bouncing here and there. Just for a moment, don't think of anything in particular; just listen to your mind. Oftentimes, I feel like an observer in a noisy room when I just listen. It is as if my memories, my hopes and dreams, and my fears are fighting for my attention the way a group of six-year-olds fight for the attention of the only adult in the room. Somewhere, hidden in that chaos, is the voice of our soul. It is usually not the loudest voice. The voice of the soul, like the many other voices, is asking for our attention to meet its needs. Many times this is a hard voice to listen to because of the truth it speaks. When we hear the voice of the soul, telling us the truth of our life, it tells us not only where it longs to go, but it also speaks of the inadequacy of where we are. I am convinced part of the reason we fill our lives with so much noise is so we can't hear the voice of our soul. Not because we don't what to hear the truth or move to where our soul longs to be, but because it is hard to hear when we are not living truth. It is easier to just lose the voice of the soul in the rumble of daily life.

To find what your soul is longing for, you will need to be quiet. You will have to live in that silence. You will have to fight to hush all the voices in your mind to hear the one of the soul. You will have to silence your own voice which is asking, *Soul, what are you saying?*—for to ask that question you must be speaking and therefore can't listen. It is important to know listening is a skill. Even if you are a good listener, you can't listen just once.

PRAYER: CALL GOD INTO THIS PROCESS

"Knock and it shall be opened. Ask and it shall be granted." Do you really believe it? I am asking you this question quite honestly. It would be very easy to say, "Bring God into the process," in any discussion. We all assume that everyone knows what that means and move on. Just for a moment I would like to challenge that notion. What do you really believe about prayer?

When I was in college I got in trouble for "using an inappropriate analogy in an academic paper". I described my frustration about how prayer is often approached. I wrote, "Prayer is not like ordering a hamburger at Happy Burger. We don't just pull up to the big clown head speaker at the drive-in and order world peace, an end to hunger, and a side of inner peace." Okay, so maybe I was a little too clever for my own good, but it does express what I think is a fallacy of prayer. We use prayer as way of placing an order with a vendor. Prayer is not a request, it is not a feeling, and it is not a prescribed set of actions and words which won't work unless they are done just right. Prayer is relationship, and like all relationships, it must be worked at.

How to Pray

If that is the case, you might be asking, "What do I need to do to really pray then? What do I really need to do to find guidance and solace from God?" That depends on who you are. I am convinced that we hear God in our personality. One of the topics I speak on quite often is my learning disabilities and the choices I have made in my life in light of those obstacles. I like the term "obstacles" much better than "disabilities". After speaking at conference in Atlanta, a high school student approached me and said, "I have ADHD just like you and I want to know how you pray. Because of the hyperactivity, I can't sit still long enough when praying to hear what God has to say." He had tapped into one of the biggest fallacies about praye, the fallacy that there is a right way we are supposed to pray. In reality there are many ways to pray. These would be called prayer styles. You might find you pray best in ritual, nature, working to fight injustice, celebration, study, music, with others, or alone. Although others have traveled this path before us and we can learn from them, still there is no set way to do it.

Right after college, I spent a month driving around the US. I stopped in St. Paul, MN to visit a friend from high school. She knew that each morning I spent some time in prayer. As I was getting ready to do this the first morning, my friend hovered around the edge of the room, patiently observing what I was up to. She was curious to see if I had cracked the code, as if I knew the magic words; that some great process was about to be revealed. Unfortunately, that is not the case. Each of us needs to find our own way.

Prayer is a very powerful force. I know that I would not have the joy that I have in my own life if I hadn't spent time in prayer. I have found true guidance in prayer. I am not a spiritual expert. I don't have theology degrees. I have never attended seminary. I am just like you, another pilgrim on the journey. If someone was to ask me, "How should I pray?" this is the advice I would provide.

IT IS A SKILL Prayer is like everything else, it is a skill. It is something I need to work at. It is no more likely that I will get a new power tool and be able to use it the moment I pick it up, than I am going to be effective in prayer the first time I do it. There have been times when I have neglected my prayer life. When I have come back, it still takes time to feel I am in communion with God.

TAKE TIME I have found that it is important in my life to take time for prayer daily. I have found I have been most fed in my prayer life when I take part in prayer daily. I can't just show up when I need something.

SACRED SPACE Sacred space is a term I have heard my whole life, but never really understood until I heard this story.

EVERY DAY A YOUNG BOY LEFT HIS FAMILY FARM (AND HIS CHORES) TO WANDER OFF TO THE WOODS. FIFTEEN MINUTES LATER HE WOULD RETURN. AFTER SEEING HIS SON DO THIS EVERYDAY FOR A NUMBER OF WEEKS, HIS FATHER BECOME CONCERNED. HE ASKED HIS BOY, "WHY DO YOU GO OFF TO THE WOODS EVERYDAY?" THE SON REPLIED, "I GO OFF TO TALK TO GOD." BUT THE FATHER PROTESTED, "GOD IS EVERY WHERE. YOU DON'T NEED TO GO TO THE WOODS TO TALK TO HIM." THE BOY, BEING WISE BEYOND HIS YEARS, KNEW THIS. HE REPLIED, "I KNOW *GOD* IS EVERY-WHERE, BUT *I* AM DIFFERENT IN THE WOODS." FIND THE PLACE THAT YOU ARE DIF-FERENT. JUST LIKE PRAYER STYLES, IT COULD BE LOTS OF PLACES.

For me, sitting quietly alone doesn't work. I get distracted by every sound. I have found my most effective prayer time is when I am a little active. When I am going for a walk, cleaning the house, doing yard work, driving on the interstate in the middle on nowhere. All of these activities that occupy my mind with some menial task (walking, cleaning, driving) allow my soul to wander where it needs to, without my mind telling it what it needs to think about. You need to find your own space.

BE HONEST If God is really God, then God knows it all already. There is no reason to hide emotion in prayer. One of my favorite parts of the Old Testament is the fact that the Jewish people always seem to be mad at God and they tell Him so. It is such an honest emotion. I know that I have been mad at God a time or two. If we don't deal with how we are feeling, we never get past it. It becomes a giant clog in our life. I grew up in Casper, WY, which is reported to have the highest average wind speed of any city in the US. One of my favorite things to do when I was growing up was to take walks at night in the wind. The beginning of my walk was always uphill into the wind. When the wind is blowing more than 30 miles an hour and it is already below zero, regardless of how many layers you are wearing, the wind cuts right through you. This is something I really enjoyed. Not because I am sick and twisted, but because when I was walking in the wind for some reason I couldn't lie. Most of the time I could lie to myself about my life, but not in that wind. The wind cut right through me. I felt like it could see inside. I could not hide the truth. The wind became a very effective tool in my prayer. It does you no good to lie to yourself about your wants and desires, or the gravity of your situation. We should be honest with where we are, especially in our prayer. It is impossible to expect an answer to a question we don't ask. In the same vein, we can't solve problems in our lives without speaking them.

PRAYER OPENS US TO POSSIBILITIES I have found in my own prayer life that when I start praying for something to be possible, I start to believe it is possible. It is no longer some distant wish. In my prayer, whatever I am praying for, I visualize it happening. I see the ways that I can start to bring my prayer into my life.

PRAY IN MANY WAYS Just as there is not "right way" to pray, there is no "right thing" to pray about. There are many types of prayer. We can offer prayers of thanksgiving, intercession, or guidance. In high school I attended a workshop on prayer. The speaker suggested that anything with God in mind is prayer. He then took it to the extreme of having us howl at the moon. Cool thought—anything we do while thinking of God is prayer. This principle is how some theologians would argue, and I would agree, our whole life can be a prayer. By being mindful of the presence of God, it becomes prayer.

How God Talks to Us

Oftentimes when I pray I make the mistake of doing all the talking and then walking away. I never listen. Mother Theresa was being interview by an American TV reporter. She was asked, "When you pray, what do you say?" Her response: "Nothing, I just listen." The reporter's interest was peaked. "Well, then, what does God say?" She said simply, "Nothing, He just listens." Cool way to describe a conversation. In the movie THE TAO OF STEVE, the main character is ranting and raving about how people always pepper God with questions and requests. One of his friends presses him to share what he says when he talks to God. The main character replies, "I ask him what he thought of Letterman last night." As silly as that seems, it points out the fact that it is dialogue we are having in prayer, not just a vent session.

If we believe that God does know everything, then it can be logically concluded that God already knows what we want and need even before we say it prayer. I also believe that in every moment of our lives God is trying to answer our prayers, but often we are unwilling to listen for those answers. Maybe it's because we are only looking for one answer in one way, or because we are not looking at all. Prayer is also important because it helps us to articulate what we think we want and it opens us up to the fact that an answer might be coming.

When God is communicating with us, *How is He doing it?* It would be very easy if every time we sat down to pray the skies would open, a giant head would appear a la MONTY PYTHON and we would hear a big booming voice. I won't say that will never happen in your life. We have a big God, who can do lots of really cool things, but this has yet to happen in my life. If it is true that God already understands our wants, desires, and vocation, and that he is trying to communicate with us, then it can be concluded that the answers to our prayers are everywhere. I believe that you can hear the answers to your prayers in dreams; in the conversation of two people next to you on the train; on a song that you can't get out of your head; in a book that has been sitting by your bed you haven't picked up for months, but for some reason you decide to today; or in the circumstances you find yourself in. If, in your prayer, you are trying to figure out what your vocation is, you have opened up yourself to listening for possibilities. Your soul is already longing for you to live your vocation. You will find when you are opened up in prayer that you are more aware of everything your soul is reacting to. That is one of the reasons that daily prayer is so important. It is as if each time you pray, you get a little better at listening—like you have cleaned a little more wax out of your ears. If you sit to pray once, you only listen once, but if you sit to pray daily then you become more and open to hear, not just in your prayer time, but all the time.

Looking for Answers

At one point a number of years ago I was feeling very unsettled. I was trying to figure out what would be the next thing I would create. It is not as if I was at a loss for ideas. I could write a book, write a comic book, start a radio show, help start another ministry, do more training with adults. I was just not sure where to go next. (Yes, please pity me. I have all of these wonderfully fun things I could do and I just can't pick. It is such a hard life.) In all of this I had been looking for guidance in prayer. I have found in my own life that when God is speaking to me, it happens in lots of different ways. Generally, it starts out very subtle, and if I don't get the hint then the messages get more and more obvious. After a few weeks it was becoming obvious that I had not been paying attention. The signals were getting very blatant and what was worse, I was still not getting the message. First, after a prayer service, I had a friend walk up to me and say, "I am not sure what you were thinking about while praying, but in my prayer I heard that I need to tell you something. It might be vague. It might be cryptic, but this is what I am supposed to say. 'You are marked for a very special ministry.'" Then, a week later, I went to the movies. After buying a ticket, I went to a newsstand to buy a candy bar before going in. As I was approaching the newsstand, a professionally dressed woman came up to me and started yelling, "You need to be more radical. Jesus was a radical and he can use radicals." My first thought in my arrogance was, "Lady, if you only knew. I live a radical life for Jesus." But then I thought, "Maybe she is trying to tell me something." For the next ten minutes I followed her around the mall at a distance. She was not yelling at anyone else.

At this point I was starting to think, "God is really trying to tell me something and I am just not getting it." I started listening to everything. Every song on the radio. Every word people said to me. Every person I passed while walking. Just listening for some message. More than likely I was listening too hard and was missing the point. As I was walking home from a coffee shop a man approached me. He was obviously drunk. I have encountered many people on the streets of DC before. I ran a homeless ministry and have lived in neighborhoods with high homeless populations. Sometimes I stop and talk, sometimes I just hand them the change they are asking for and move on. There are sometimes where I just say "sorry." As I approached this man he stuck out his hand to shake. My first thought was, "Maybe this guy is an angel. Maybe he has a message for me." I stopped and shook his hand. I just listened openly, as openly as I have ever listened in my life. His name was Lee (or so he claimed). He asked for some help. I gave him two bucks. We talked about my blue hair. He said he was off to buy a beer. He gave me a hug and that was it. No earth shattering message for my life. I did not walk away depressed, but instead my first thought was, "I just approached this man as if he was an angel. I gave him my undivided attention because I thought he was a messenger from God." When we are traveling and on stage, I always say that we are all loved children of God and that we are the Body of Christ. For one of the first times in my life I truly understood what that meant. Lee was an angel. He was a messenger from God, in the same way every one of us is as well. I can't even imagine what life would be like if I approached everyone as the messenger of God that they are. That is how we open ourselves up to hear response to our prayer, because it is everywhere.

One Other Way Prayers Are Answered

How prayers are answered varies as much as the styles in which we pray, but there was one final story I wanted to offer about prayers—to illustrate that one way prayers are answered, is within us. I was visiting my friend Jason in San Diego. The first night I was in town we headed down to the beach for Chinese food. We sat on the top of a small cliff overlooking the beach and the ocean. Before starting to eat, Jason said grace. The last line, "Please be with all those who will never know a meal this fine." The line really struck me. I had prayed for those who had less than me before, but I had never really given the quality of my food consideration.

Two days later, we were on the way to the church where Jason volunteered with the junior high youth group. On the way, Jason asked if it was okay if we made a stop. No big deal. Well, it turned out that the stop we made was at a soup kitchen in which every week he personally bought all the food that was served and then helped serve it. Besides being a noble act, it taught me a great lesson about prayer. Jason understood that he was part of the answer of the prayer for helping those without food. He didn't just send up a request to some distant God, but understood that he is the Body of Christ in the world.

I have found, time and again, in my own life that my prayers become answered when I start working towards having them answered. One of my favorite descriptions of "knock and it shall be opened" is "when you ask for something, the whole universe conspires to make it so." I think of all the times in which a "coincidence" helped something to work out. That "coincidence" (read "actual grace") would have done me no good if I hadn't been looking for it or trying to head in the right direction. The universe conspiring to have our desires come true is a very powerful force, but we must participate in that, for the universe can't do it alone.

WHAT WE NEED AND WHAT WE HAVE

Eighteen hours before I departed for Northern Ireland to visit my friend Molly, I received a phone message. "Gene, this is Molly's mother. Molly is in the hospital and will be there for the next three weeks. She hopes you have a good trip."

I had made no plans for the trip. I was going to a country where I spoke the language and had a friend who lived there waiting for me. There was no reason to plan. All of a sudden, I was the accidental tourist. I knew the town Molly was in, and the name of the organization she worked for, not much more. I figured I'd go find her. On the flights to Dublin I read a travel guide (which I had bought on the way to airport) cover to cover. In that time I had figured out how to get to the train station downtown, which train to catch, and where to look in Belfast for a hostel to stay the night before I continued to the northern coast. Before boarding the train, I wandered into a bakery for some tea and light snack. I ended up with two scones. If you have never had scones before, they are really nothing more than biscuits (in this case with raisins). I ate one and put the other in my backpack. I made it to Belfast easily enough, and the first hostel I tried had a bed. After a long day of travel I crashed.

I woke up at 2AM. Who knows what time my body thought it was. I was very hungry. As my eyes began to focus in the darkened room I realized I was no longer alone. The other five beds in the room were now full of resting travelers. As quietly as I could, I climbed out of my bunk and left the room. I went down to the kitchen to see if I could find some food. In the fridge was a can of coffee and some catsup. Not feeling bold enough in my new surroundings to wander the street to find food (generally a good thought in a foreign country), I figured I would just have to suck it up until morning. Then I remember I had one scone in my backpack.

I knew where I had put my backpack the night before, so on my belly, army style, I slithered across the bedroom floor, grabbed the scone and fled back to the hallway. I sat on the floor leaning up against wall. I slowly unwrapped the scone. I no longer had a thirty-five cent piece of bread in my hand. I now had the Bread of Life itself. I am sure this is exactly how the manna in desert tasted. I was certain this scone had been crafted by the finest baker in all of Ireland. I ate slowly, enjoying every bite (even going so far as to lick the crumbs of the paper it was wrapped with). It tasted so good because it was enough. It was what I needed. Not what I needed for the whole trip. It was what I needed for the night.

How Much More Do You Need?

We were performing in Cincinnati, and instead of staying at a hotel, we chose to stay with friends. Sean was giving us the tour of his family's home. It is a beautiful old home. It has a large porch and all hardwood floors. A home like the one I would like to own someday. When they had bought the home, like many older homes, it needed a lot of work. As we were walking through the house getting the tour Sean took us into the laundry room. Like all the rooms on the first floor it had a ten-foot ceiling. One of the walls was painted to about eight feet high. The paint did not end in a clean line as if it was planned to end there. Instead, it looked as if was painted as high as a person could reach. Sean pointed to that spot on the wall and said, "This is where I stopped building my house and started building the kingdom." It was obvious Sean understood what his family needed. They needed a nice house to keep them warm, safe, and comfortable. Sean saw it as more important to do the work his faith was imploring him to do (build the Kingdom of God) than to make the most functional room of the house look pretty.

We live in a culture which tells us over and over again that we need more, that we need better, but I don't think that is always true. I own twelve pairs of shoes. I don't need twelve pairs of shoes. Is it fun to be able to mix and match my outfits (I think this is the first time I have ever used the word "outfit" in this context in my life) with my different pairs of shoes. In the end, I can only wear one pair of shoes at a time. I know there are things in my life more important than having that many pairs of shoes. It is important to understand how much we need.

Guilt and Gratitude

In Ecuador, part of the bus culture is to have people constantly getting on and off the bus selling stuff. This happens in two ways. One way is what I would call the meditative chant. Someone would jump on the bus, hold their goods up in the air, and say what they had and the cost over and over in a complete monotone voice. "Chicle, diez centavos. Chicle, diez centavos. Chicle, diez centavos. Chicle, diez centavos..." "Gum, ten cents." The second method was the *this is my life* method. The salesperson would pass out one of everything they were trying to sell to everyone on the bus, then return to the front of the bus and start their story. "Hello, my name is Juan. I have fourteen brothers and sisters. I am trying to pay my way to school...."

In the month I lived in Ecuador I rode the bus daily, and so these salespeople became part of the fabric of ride as much as the ranchero music that was always playing. In all my bus rides there were only two notable exceptions to these two sales techniques. The first was a pen salesman, who should have had a job on an infomercial. He had all the shtick and cadence of someone selling on TV at two in the morning. Right down to the phrases, "Would you pay a dollar for this pen? Before you answer, there is more! This pen is so versatile you can use it at home, at work, on vacation, and even at the beach." He really said that, in Spanish of course.   "I am offering this pen, this pencil, this eraser, this bottle of glue, and this marker that writes in eight colors. Would you pay five dollars? Would you pay three dollars? Would you pay two dollars? You don't have to. You can have all of this for just one dollar." The other North Americans I was traveling with and I just lost it. It was wonderful. We all bought pen sets which had pictures of Korean pop stars on them, a feature that had not been pointed out, but was definitely a bonus.

The second exception was a small boy selling cookies. We were on the bus on our way to Sacasili for the outdoor market. At the edge of Quito, a boy of about ten or eleven got on the bus, walked down the aisle handing each of us two packets of cookies. He returned to the front of the bus. Instead of talking about his life or the cookies he was trying to sell, he pulled out a bag of candy and said, *(translated)* "I am going to ask five questions. If you get a question right I will give you a piece of candy. The last question is much harder. If you get that right, I will give you two pieces of candy. Question number one: What is the name of an animal which has a very long neck?"

Obviously, the answer is a giraffe, but in my four-week introduction to the Spanish language that was not a vocabulary word I had encountered. Odd that my teachers didn't see that was an important word for me to know but for some reason I did know the verb meaning "to dye fabric".

I didn't understand the second question. "The third question I have is this: Which direction is the bus going?" People start yelling out "South!" "East!" "Southeast!" All good answers, but not right for some reason. Then people just start guessing. "North!" "West!" Finally someone yelled, "Forward!" *Perfecto!* They win candy.

"My fourth question: On what side of the grocery store do you find the milk?"

"The right!" "The left!" "The East!" Lots of answers but none right. "No, I am sorry, milk is found on the inSIDE.

"The fifth and final question: An airplane is flying from Columbia to Ecuador and it collides with another airplane right on the boarder of the two countries. Where do you bury the survivors?" Again, I know the answer, but have no idea how to say, "Nowhere. You don't bury survivors."

The whole presentation was very clever. Not only did the kid have good material, he was a great performer, great timing and moxie. He was very poised in front of a crowd of adults who were used to having people try to sell them cookies and candy they didn't want. I could only imagine what this kid would grow up to be if he lived in the US—a comedian...an actor...me? More than likely he will spend his life trying to make ends meet selling stuff on the bus. As I sat there on the bus, eating the cookies I didn't need but had just bought, the moment gave me a real moment of pause. I live such a wonderful life. My business partner Brad and I get to take the gifts and talents we have been given, and marry them to work we love. We travel all over the US and Canada sharing our faith and making people laugh. We work hard at our craft and I don't think anything has just been given to us. We have worked hard to get where we are, but our success is not solely a function of our hard work. Much of what we have is because of where we started. We had no say in the fact that we were born in a country that gave us great opportunity. We had no control over the wonderful families we were born into who continue to encourage us and give us support. We have worked hard, but we have also been given so much. We have blessed lives.

By the simple fact that you have picked up this book, you live a blessed life too. You had enough money to buy the book. You have the free time to read the book. You have obtainable goals to reach for. We are all aware of the suffering there is in the world. For the most part, our daily lives do not have us in direct contact with abject poverty, but we know it is there. It is very easy to be consumed with guilt because of the choices we have. I know in my own life this has happened a number of times. When I'm volunteering someplace or on a mission trip I have no choice but to confront how much I really have. The job I have is one of *many* jobs I could have and it is something I have *chosen* to do because I enjoy it. When I was on that bus in Ecuador, I realized that if I had been born somewhere else I might be performing to feed my family or worse, not having a chance to use my giftedness at all.

There is suffering in this world, and it happens in all walks of life. Many times we can't understand that those that have more than us would suffer. The chorus of the Good Charlotte song LIFESTYLES OF THE RICH AND FAMOUS sings, "If money is such a problem, why don't we rob them." More and more studies are being done on the effect of material wealth on true happiness. Study after study shows that there is little or no connection between the two. I am not saying a CEO who is suffering from depression because he is stuck in work that is sucking away his life and his joy, in exchange for being handsomely compensated, is feeling the same as someone who is starving to death, but there is suffering everywhere.

The only suffering we know is the suffering of our experience. Guilt is debilitating. If you feel guilty over the choice you have to make, you will become paralyzed and will not be able to make a choice at all. On the other hand, recognizing what you have and regretting that others are suffering can be a motivation toward acting in a way that reflects your values. We live blessed lives. The circumstance we find ourselves in right now is a combination of choices and the hand that we have been dealt. In most cases, we can't give our lives or our choices to someone else, but it does us very little good to feel guilty. Instead the blessing we have been given is a challenge and a responsibility. One of the ways we can show that we are thankful for those blessings is to make our choices carefully and prayerfully. We steward these blessing by handling our lives with care. Our thanksgiving is using what we have been given. This is what our soul is longing for. It is when we are following our vocation that we are using all the great blessing we have been given. We are showing thanks for those blessings in the lives we live.

PART III

Crafting a Life of Passion

It's time to craft the narrative of your life of passion. This not to say, that when you finish this section you are going to have that done, but what follows is the first steps. You are also going to do a little dreaming to imagine what your perfect life could look like as well as look at your life to this point. From this information, you are going to be able to craft a vision for what your life can look like in eight different areas. From this you will create an action plan. Finally, we will look at some of the perils and pitfall, for dream chasing and living a life of passion. A number of these activities are not going to feel like they have anything to do with crafting a life you can live with passion. Trust the process.

A few notes before you being. Remember this is a process. It is much more art than it is science. There is no formula. You are not going to plug data and have your perfect life come out the other side. Second, this is going to take time. You won't be able to do this section of the book in one sitting. Some of the activities are going to take a few days of thought. Finally, have fun with this part of the book. There are a number of activities in which you get to let your imagination run wild. Some of the activities are going to feel a little childish, that is by design. When we look at the world as a child, sometimes we see things in a new way. All of this will be to our advantage. With that being said, it is time to begin to work of crafting the life you can live with passion.

GATHERING INFORMATION

The activities in this section fall into two groups. They will either look at the experiences of your life or look to your dreams for the future. In both of these places, you can find clues about a life you can live with passion. As you do these activities, put the final goal out of your mind. Don't try to figure out why you are doing any particular activity. This first step is only about collecting information. In the second step, you will spend time sifting through the information to find what it means. Each time you sit-down to do some work, make sure you do a warm-up activity or two, and then dive right into the activity. Don't worry if you are writing down the right or the most useful information. Get out your notebook and just go for it. If you approach each activity with an open mind, the information you create will be much more useful for the work of the second step.

Warm-up Activities: Art of Creativity

I was recently visiting my godson Jack and his parents. Jack is two years old, so unless he is watching BROTHER BEAR or sleeping, he needs constant attention. Really, it is not that he needs the attention, but the house needs protection. His parents needed to work on something together, so they asked if I would keep an eye on him, which I love doing. I sat down at the kitchen table where he was drawing, picked up a marker and started to draw. Well, no, not exactly. I picked up a marker and starting thinking about what I was going to draw. Jack, on the other hand, was facing no similar obstacle. The only time he was not drawing was when he was switching from one color to the next. Otherwise it was a constant sweeping of motion. He wasn't thinking what he should draw, or what the best way to draw was. He was simply drawing. It wasn't thoughtless either, because he was amazed at his own work.

For most of us, somewhere along the way, the inner artist dies. We turn into beings that must use plan and reason. We need to find a way to bring that artist back. Not that plan and reason are all bad. We are going to use a lot of that here. I am sure you have encountered someone who could be called a "flaky artist," who is in touch with their inner artist, but can't remember where they put their car keys, what day it is, or if they have had lunch yet. We need to find a balance. Discovering your dream is art. Executing a life you can live with passion takes a plan. We have to do both.

Every time you sit down to do one of the activities in this section, you are going to need to spend a little time warming up the inner artist inside of you. In order to warm up your inner artist, you should do one of these warm-up activities. These activities are going to seem a little silly (or a lot silly, based on your point of view). What you will have on your paper at the end of the activity will look a little odd. The goal of the activities is not what ends up on paper, but the fact that you are using your inner artist. Warming up your inner artist will make it much easier to listen to what your soul is calling for.

WARM UP 1: WORD ASSOCIATION
- In the top left corner of a blank piece of paper, write any word.
- Under the word, write the first word that comes to mind. Don't spend time thinking about what word to write. There is no right answer. Just write quickly. (Example: If you start with the word "banana" you might write the word "peel.")
- Under the second word, write the first word that comes to mind. (Example: "peel" is followed by the word "skin.")
- Continue adding words down the page.
- When you reach the bottom of the page, move back to the top and start a new column.
- Continue until you have six completed columns
- Go back and re-read your columns.

WARM UP 2: FREE DRAW
- Get a blank sheet of paper and a bunch of writing utensils (pens, pencils, crayons, markers)
- In the center of the page start drawing. Don't think about what to draw. Just draw. If you are not sure what to draw, just start moving your pen.
- As you continue to draw, just follow where the pen leads you.
- The only time you should not be drawing is when you are switching colors.
- Draw nonstop for ten minutes
- Spend a little time exploring what you have just drawn.

Note: *If you are feeling self-conscious about what you are drawing, remember the goal of the activity is to get your inner artist moving. The goal is not to draw a pretty picture. You don't have to show the drawing to anyone when you are done. Don't hesitate. Just draw.*

WARM UP 3: FREE WRITE
- On a blank piece of paper, start writing. Write about anything. You can write about what you are feeling. How stupid you think this exercise is. You can write about your dream last night. Write about anything.
- Keep writing no matter what. If you can't think of anything to write, write "I can't think of anything to write." Whatever comes into your mind, put it down on the piece of paper.
- Write non-stop for ten minutes.
- Re-read what you have written.

WARM UP 4: LOOKING AT THE CLOUDS
- Go outside and lay on your back and look at the clouds.
- For 10 minutes figure out what the clouds look like.
- It is even better if you can do this activity with a 6-year-old.

What We Have

Ask anyone how their day was and more often than not you'll get a list of all the things that have gone wrong. The bad traffic, the rude customer service, or the spaghetti sauce that ruined their favorite shirt. Occasionally, someone will give a balanced report, generally with the problems listed first. Every so often you will get a positive report, but this generally comes only after an extraordinary day. I think of myself as very optimistic person, but still have a tendency to complain much more than I should.

I believe one of the steps to living a passionate life is to understand what we already have. We spend so much time thinking about fixing the problems in our lives (which we should fix) and thinking about all that we want to become, we often neglect to notice what we already have. Many of us have much more joy in our lives than we realize. We simply fail to recognize it. One of the people who inspired me to become a speaker is a man by the name of Lee Nagel. I only met Lee once when I was in high school. He was a speaker at a youth rally I attended. He was funny, inspiring, and off-stage was very present to everyone who wanted a moment of his time. I have heard a story about something Lee does daily (or did daily at one point in his life). The story goes that every day Lee sends ten thank you notes—let me repeat, everyday—the reason being, that there are at least ten things you need to be thankful for every day. I start my day by writing a list of ten things I am thankful for. This might be overkill, but if you are aware of all the things you have in your life for which you should be thankful, you start to understand the richness that you already have in your life.

Before we start to make a plan for what we would like to transform our lives into, I think it is important to understand what we have. Make a few lists of the things you are thankful for in all parts of your life. Understand what is good about your friends, family, the work you do, your health, and your leisure time. In theological terms, we understand God is everywhere in all things. We have moments of "actual grace" when we recognize God's presence. When you see a stunning sunset and give thanks to God, that is actual grace. When we see a small child learn something new, and marvel at the way life grows and develops, that is actual grace. God is always there, but we don't always realize it. Taking time to give thanks for what is in our lives will help you to see the grace and joy your life is always filled with. When we are consciously thankful, we are more aware of what we already have and spend less time longing for more.

GIVING THANKS
- On a blank piece of paper in your notebook, write the following headings with five lines between each one. Spirituality, Immediate Family (only add this if you are married or have children), Friends and Family, Education, Personal Health, Personal Finance, Work, and Leisure.
- Under each heading, add five things that you are thankful for.

Note: *In some of these areas, it will be hard to come up with five items. It is important that you come up with five, because there are more than five items you should be thankful for in each area.*

What Brings and Seals Joy

Now that you have spent a little time looking at what you are thankful for in your life, I would like to continue to look at what brings you happiness and joy, as well at what steals happiness and joy out of your life. You will make some lists about your life. This exercise is going to take some time. Not because it is complicated, but because it requires the type of thinking that makes you mull over your life. You are going to make two lists. One of the lists will be of everything you can think of that makes you happy or brings you joy. The other list will be of all the things and experiences that steal joy from your life. These lists should include everything. List the big and the small. If you love playing with your kids, write it down. If you love getting foot massages, write it down. I even want you to include the things you think might bring you joy, like visiting the town in Italy where your grandmother was born. I don't want you to make any value judgments about the list. The same thing is true for things that steal your life and your joy away from you. Again, the big and the small. If someone who cuts you off gets you hot under the collar, write it down. If not being valued for the work you do hurts you, write it down. Do this for three or four days. Carry the lists with you everywhere you go. You will be amazed at all the things that strike you. Don't think to yourself, "It is not important. I shouldn't write it down." That is not the case. We need them all. No one item or activity is going to hold the answer to shaping the life you want, but all of the little pieces are going to give us clues.

GIVING AND SEALING JOY

- On one piece of paper in your notebook, make a list of all the things and activities that give joy to your life. Also, include things you think you might like to do.
- On a second page, make a list of all the things and activities that steal joy from your life. These items should include the big and the small.
- Carry the lists with you for at least three days, adding items whenever they come to mind.
- Each list should have at least 150 items.

Notes: *Don't make value judgments, thinking something is too small to be added. Add everything that comes to mind.*

Small Steps to Bring Joy to Your Life

It is important to note that what we have just done is only one step in the process. Finding our vocation is not as easy as just listing what we love and what we don't. Years ago, I was working with a very bright high school student, helping her try and figure out what she wanted to do with her life (at least in the near term). After doing this exercise Ryan said, "This is great, but it is not as easy as playing basketball, eating Wavy Gravy ice cream, and avoiding my dad." She is right. It is not that easy, but this is start. What it does is helps us to understand how the people and experiences in our lives affect us. Even if you don't follow the process all the way to its natural conclusion, by simply recognizing the ways different things affect you, you can bring more joy into your life (and in some cases get rid of things that are killing your joy).

For example, I was working with a couple. As they were going through this process with me, they named the fact that they really loved spending time together, just the two of them. This is not unusual for two people in love. What was also not unusual was the fact that they had two kids, 6 and 4, who required their time and care. Not only was it hard to get time together, but when they would get an intimate moment together, it was late and they were both so tired, it was more like quiet time next to eachother than time with each other. So part of their plan, like many couples, was to create a date night once a week. They would take the kids over to the grandparents, and the night was theirs. Nothing too revolutionary at this point. Good ideas don't have to be revolutionary. They added one twist. Part of their goal was to spend one hour of their date-night time making love. It was something they had both named as important in their relationship, being able to truly be present and intimate with each other. Later when they reported back, I received more details than I am sure I needed. They said that many weeks they didn't make the full hour, and sometimes they just ended up holding each other in their arms, just talking. One thing was for certain: realizing how important time together (alone) was, and making it happen, improved their quality of life. For the cost of time and attention, they had more joy.

If I Ever Grow Up

For whatever reason, as we grow older, it becomes harder and harder to listen to our souls. Our days and minds get filled with the noise of the world, so there is less and less room left to hear our souls. Our thoughts are monopolized by over-packed schedules; we don't just seem to sit and listen. I know there are times that I have longed for a simpler time, when the greatest problem was trying to round up enough kids to play hide and seek. Think back to that time. Long summer nights. Bike rides that filled the whole day. Games that required nothing more than a stick and little imagination. Even if you didn't know it, you could hear your soul much more clearly then. Think back to that time. What did you want to be when you grew up? Also, ask why you wanted to be that. Go back and ask the first grade 'you', "What do you want to be when you grow up?" Do it for the second grade 'you', and the third, and so on. Don't lament the loss of those dreams. Don't believe this is what you are supposed to be doing with your life. As a fourth grader in Wyoming I wanted to be a Marine Biologist. I am certain that is not in my future. But there are more clues in those childhood dreams. Just listen to the truth the child within you is speaking.

WHEN I GROW UP
- On a blank piece of paper in your notebook, write the numbers one through twelve.
- After each number, write what you wanted to be when you grew up and why for the grade that corresponds with the number.

Note: *If at one point you wanted to be lots of things (like an astronaut/actress/princess) write them all down. If you wanted to be the same thing a number of years in a row, write down for each year it is applicable.*

Remember Me?

Recently, for an article written about our ministry, the reporter wanted to interview people who had known us for a while to get some background on us. It was interesting to read the recollections of the people who knew me in high school. To be honest, at that point in my life I really couldn't see beyond the nose at the end of my face, much less give much thought what others thought about me. Today, I give it a little more thought—not to the point where I am shaping my actions so I am acceptable to the world at large—but in my more reflective moments, I wonder if my actions reflect the words I speak. How do I want to be remembered? I often find this a helpful question when I am getting worked up over something. In the scope of my life, am I going to remember it and are others going to remember it about me? Spend some time thinking about how you want to be remembered. For this, think in terms of characteristics (generous, faithful) and specific (help create a great team environment at work).

REMEMBERED

- On a blank sheet of paper in your notebook make a list of the characteristics and activities you want to be remembered for. List things that you do now and thing you would like to do with your life.

Sweet Memories

Growing up, my family did lots of traveling. No doubt, where my travel bug first started. Most of the time, because of cost, we drove. Calling Wyoming home meant very long car trips, usually taking more than one day to get anywhere. On one of our trips to the West Coast we stopped for an overnight in Beaver, Utah. Beaver is a small town, and we found ourselves staying at a small, family-run motel. Right in front of the hotel, there was a large, grassy hill with a duck pound at the bottom. I have three distinct memories of the hotel. First, using the Magic Fingers in the hotel room. Magic Fingers was a machine which was part of the bed. If you put a dime into the box on the nightstand the bed would start vibrating, giving you a full body massage...sort of. I didn't know how it worked. After I put my dime in the machine, I put my hand on the little box on the night stand thinking it would vibrate my fingers, thus shaking my whole body. I was twelve and hadn't been out of Wyoming much. Give me a break. Second, it was a beautiful evening and we picnicked on the grassy hill. The picnic was topped off with my mom's homemade chocolate chip cookies. Third, after dinner we spent time rolling down the hill. As we were doing this, my sister managed to roll right into a duck pond (a story which is told over and over by my family).

I could not tell you where we were heading on the trip (other than west). It is one of those perfect nights that just sticks out for my family and me. I am sure it is a night I will remember fondly forever. We weren't doing anything but being together, being family. So often when we try and script our lives, we try to fill them with stuff and "exceptional" experiences. Years later those are not the things we remember. It is the simple times of joy that remain.

Imagine you are at your 90th birthday party. You are surrounded by loved ones. You and the family are just chatting about the good ol' days. What is the life you would like to remember? I am not talking about what has really happened to you up to this point. Forty years from now, how are you remembering the next forty years of your life?

MEMORIES
- On a blank sheet of paper, create a list of the memories of the past that you would like to have forty years from now.

Haven't You Always Wanted a Monkey?

The Canadian band, The Barenaked Ladies, sing longingly about all the wonderful things they would do with lots of money in their popular song IF I HAD A MILLION DOLLARS. They would buy a house, they wouldn't have to walk to the store, and they would end up buying a monkey. All together now sing, "Haven't you always wanted a monkey?" I know I have lived the fantasy of winning the lottery. Dreaming it would make all my problems go away. Intellectually, I understand (1) it is not going to happen—I don't buy lottery tickets—and (2) it wouldn't make all my problems go away. With that being said, it is a good fantasy to ponder when we consider what our lives could look like. What would you do if you won five million dollars after taxes? What would you buy for yourself? Your family? Me? Who would you give money to? Where would you travel? Imagine it is a BREWSTER'S MILLIONS situation (a Richard Pryor movie from the eighties). You have one year to spend all the money. Any money that is not spent or given away is taken back.

FIVE MILLION DOLLARS
- On a blank sheet of paper in your notebook, write down everything you would do if you had one year to spend five million dollars.

Extended Vacation

Every year, Brad and I get the opportunity to work with the senior class at a high school in Charlotte, NC. One of my favorite parts of the two days we spend with them, is sitting in on small-group discussion and having meals with the students. I am curious to hear of their plans for the future. I also find is fascinating to hear them talk about the pressures that shape what they think their future should look like. Pressures from parents, friends, and the pressure they put on themselves for success (whatever success is). You can hear in their stories, and often in their voices—the way that many of them are trying to live a definition of success that they don't believe in. The question that I have found very useful in helping them figure out what they want is, "If you had a one-year vacation, where money is no object, what would you do with your time?" Now after I convince them that sitting on a beach would start to lose its luster after a week or two, much less the six months they want to spend there, they start to open up the possibilities of what they really want. A few of them would still choose school, but most won't. When I press why, many feel they just don't know what they really want in their lives, and choosing a certain course doesn't seem right. So, how about you? You have a one-year vacation starting today. Money is no object. What do you do with the time? Where do you go? With whom? Why?

ONE-YEAR VACATION
- On a blank piece of paper in your notebook, describe how you would spend the next year of your life if you could anything you wanted and money was no object.

Your Resources

The next step in the process is to understand where you are right now. In purely financial terms what you have are your assets. So what you are going to do now is make three lists of all the assets you have, but you are going to make the list not in financial terms. The three types of assets you are to list are your time, talents, and treasure. If you have ever been through a stewardship campaign before, I am sure you have heard these words in this context. They make sense in this context. You are trying to get joy into your life, and time, talent, and treasure is what you have to spend. You are going to make a list of each type. First a brief word on each.

TIME Your time column is going to be short. We all have the same amount of time. We have 168 hours a week. So under the heading of time, write 168 hours. You might think to yourself, "I don't really have 168 hours a week. I have to sleep and go to work. Those are not hours I have." They are hours you have. Sleeping is just one of the ways you choose to spend them (and a very good way, I might add). In the next step, we will get to all the ways you spend your time. For now all we want are your assets—in this case: 168 hours a week.

TALENTS This is a list of everything you can do, and I don't mean this in purely a work context. I don't even mean it in the way that we generally think of skills. I mean everything you are good at. If you are good at making web pages, write it down. If you are good at fixing toilets, write it down. If you are really good at making your daughter smile when she is having a rough day, write it down. This list you're making is of everything that you have to offer the world. This is what you have to spend in order to get joy into your life. This is one of the most diffi-cult lists you will be asked to make. Most of us are modest about our abilities. Many of us are so modest we can't recognize the things we are good at. You are not bragging in this exercise. This is not the list you are showing to the world. Just as it was important before that you were honest with yourself about the reality of the struggles in your life, now you need be honest to list everything you are good at.

This list is different than the list of things you like to do. It is okay to spend time on things you are not good at. Playing golf might be on your list of things you like to do, but with your 28 handicap it is hard to say you are good at it. Though, making your father-in-law laugh every time you play might be something you are good at.

TREASURE This is nothing more than a list of everything you own that has value. List your house, your car, family heirlooms, stamp collections, life insurance that you have, pension plans, savings, stock portfolios, and anything else that you have of value. When you make this list, it is important to be specific about what you are listing and how much each item is worth. Don't list how much you bought it for, but what it is now worth. Find the blue book value of your cars. Use the most current estimate on your house. More than likely if you have picked up this book, this list is going to be very short, but that is okay. Remember, the best time to plant a tree is 20 years ago, the second best time is right now. Right? Sure, it would have been better if you had started working on building your assets years ago, but that doesn't matter. What matters is that you are starting now.

There is one final note you want to consider with each of your assets: how long will you have these assets? I am not talking about how long you will own your car, but if there is time sensitivity to any of your assets. You have 24 hours today. No matter how you choose to spend them, you have to spend them. You can't make time stop. You might choose to spend your afternoon playing solitaire with your seven hundred dollar deck of cards (no, wait, I mean computer). That isn't the best way to spend your time, but it is time you spent nonetheless. Make a notation next to each of the items that are time sensitive (things that will not be here forever). Time is the most obvious item that is time sensitive, but also consider the skills you have. Some skills you will retain your whole life, while others, because of their physical nature, you might no longer enjoy as you get older.

WHAT YOU HAVE
- Label three blank sheets of paper in your notebook with the titles "Time", "Talent", and "Treasure".
- In the left-hand column on each page, write down every asset you have that fits the category.
- Leave a line or two between each asset you name.
- Go through each list at least twice. The first time through the list, think in terms of "What assets do I have?" The second time you work through the list think of what you have accomplished in the last few months, big and small, and ask, "What assets did I use in these situations to be successful?"
- Use multiple pages for Talents and Treasures if necessary.
- After your list are complete mark all the assets that are time sensitive

Notes: *Remember to think as broadly as possible, not just in terms of marketable skills. Think of assets that you have not used in years. On the page for Time, at this point you will only have 168 hours listed in the left-hand column.*

Using Your Resources

It is time to look at how you are using the assets you have. This is going to serve two purposes. First, it will show you how many different types of activities you do well. Second, it will help you to identify all of the assets that you have that you are not utilizing. The most glaring waste of assets in most people's lives is the time they have. It is amazing how much time we spend watching TV we really don't want to watch. Much of moving towards living a life with passion, is getting a handle on the waste we have in our lives. Go through each of the assets that you have and identify how you are using each one. With many assets you are going to be able to think of more than just one example of where you use a particular asset. You might use a particular asset in multiple situations. One of your talents might be building teams. That might manifest itself in your life at work, in your family, and with your church council. Be as specific as possible. The answer "at work" is not enough. Write something like "I am able to get my co-workers to see and understand each other's opinions."

In this section, the hardest asset to track is your time. I know I can't think back to last weekend and tell you how many hours I spent watching TV, how long it took me to mow the lawn, and how many hours I slept. The more time you spend on this section, the more accurate it will be, and the more helpful will be in seeing how you waste your time. The two recommendations I would offer to filling out this page would be these. The easiest would be this: before bed at night, think back on how you spent your time that day. Include everything. Your time should add up to 24 hours each day. Include sleep and work. The second approach is a little more time-consuming (and you might feel a little silly), but it is much more accurate and will be more helpful. Every hour of the day, write down how you spent the last hour. When I have done this in the past, I have worn my digital watch and had it count down from an hour over and over. Every time the watch went off, I would write down what I had done in the last hour. (No, I did not let the watch run all night. I figured I was able to do the math after I woke up to see how many hours I had slept). Once you have collected a week's worth of data, start adding the time into categories. For example: 55 hours working, 5 hours commuting, 58 hours sleeping (I wish), 18 hours watching TV, 4 hours running the kids to activities. The more meticulous you are in keeping track of your time and the categories the time is placed into, the more helpful the data will be.

SPENDING YOUR ASSETS

- In the right hand column on your three pages of assets, write how you use each of your assets.
- If you use one asset in more than one setting, write down each use.
- Be as specific as possible.

Note: *It is possible that you will have assets that you are not using as all.*

Stories of our lives

At my core, I am a storyteller. I love telling stories. It really brings me joy. The stories I know best and can tell the best are the ones that are about me. I know it is hard to believe that I like telling stories about myself. (Please note the author's sarcasm of the last statement.) Because I am a storyteller for a living, I need to have lots of stories on hand. Most of the time when we are at conferences, the stories we tell are predetermined. We know the age group and theme ahead of time. From years of performing, we have a pretty good idea of what is going to work. Sometimes, things just don't go as planned. For whatever reason, there needs to be a change. For example we have miscalculated the nature of the event or some event has happened that was unexpected that we need to respond to (like a flood destroying 14 classrooms while we were on stage). In

order to prepare for that situation, over a number of weeks, I spent time each day thinking of stories that have happened in my life. I thought of all phases of my life. At first I wasn't looking for stories with a moral to them. I have found it is more
important to have a good story than an okay story with a moral. One of the reasons it is a good story is because it contains some truth. It is a good story because the listener can relate to the story, the truth it contains. So my task was to find the good stories in my life. After that I tried to imagine a situation in which I might be able to use those stories on stage. By having all these stories in my hip pocket, they (and I) were ready when needed.

Going through this process, I made an amazing discovery (at least it was a discovery to me). The stories we tell are not the truth. That is not to say they don't contain truth we can learn from, or that they are not based in fact, but they are not true is so far as telling what really happened. If you doubt me, have three of your family members tell the same story. All three of you will have different details; some details that you will disagree on will be very significant details. For example, a high school student came up to me after we had done an evening of stories at his church. He told me that I had told the story wrong. He insisted that the last time we were there I had told the same story in a different way. The thing was, the story I was telling was about my own life, a story I have told hundreds of times, and the facts as he remembered them made the story completely implausible.

It is okay that the stories we tell are not what really happened, but they do tell us something more than just the events as we remember them. The stories we tell (at least the ones about our lives) either tell us who we think we were, who we think we are, or who we would like to be. When we tell stories we are providing witness to some idea, and the witness is the lives we have lived.

Imagine that you have just received a call from a biographer who wants to write about you. She is going to come over to your house in one week and would like to hear you talk about your life. What stories would you tell? Think about all parts of your life. What are the stories that come to mind? Who are the characters you have interacted with? After you have thought of these stories, what is it that we can learn about you from your stories? I believe in these stories, you can find hints of your dream and beliefs. These are stories that can help guide you to knowing what you want in your life. Possible types of stories to consider are: a triumph, a lost love, a hard lesson, first love, a childhood memory, a loving friend, getting lost, or a great mentor.

STORIES OF YOUR LIFE
- Make a list of all of the stories of your life you would like to share with your biographer. Start with your earliest memories and work forward through each part of your life.
- For each story, write a brief synopsis of the story and all the significant characters of your life.

Outside Input

It is very helpful to ask others for input. Sometimes we are so wrapped up in our own lives, we don't have a clear vision of what is going on. Our loved ones can have helpful information about our lives. Of all of the steps in this process, this is the most delicate. First, you are going to open yourself up to praise and critique. You need to make sure that you are able to hear what is going to be said about you and not take it personally (because what others are going to say *is* about you). Know that if you ask others to be candid about you, then they will be. If you asked someone to look at your life critically, it is not fair to then hold it against them when they tell you the truth they see. Second, you need to ask for input from people who know you well and whom you trust. Asking a co-worker who you have known for three months, probably isn't going to provide you a lot of insight. Your siblings are going to know you better. Third, it is important to understand that everyone who you ask for help is going to have a bias as well. Just because they are on the outside doesn't mean they are going to see you more clearly; it just means they are going to see you with a different perspective. The answers you get are just more data that you are going to process. It is important to remember that this is more input, not *the* best or *the* most accurate input. For example, if you ask your mother what she thinks your life calling is, she might say wife and mother. This may be because that is what she sees, or it might be because that is her definition of a successful woman in the world and that is what she wants for you, but not necessarily sees in you.

There are a number of simple things you can do to ensure you get the best possible data from others. First, before for you set up time to talk with someone, let them know exactly what type of input you are looking for ahead of time. This will give them a chance to process. Second, set aside a large chunk of time. You don't want the process to be rushed. If you can meet face to face, that works best. Third, when you meet, ask them to describe your strengths, your weaknesses, how they would describe you to others, and what they think might be your calling in life. Again, they are not giving you answers, just input. Finally, have the conversation with a number of people. It is not necessary to do this with fifty people, but the input of four or five trusted people in your life will be helpful.

OUTSIDE INPUT
- When contacting people for input, make sure you explain what you are looking for and why you are doing it.
- Consider giving them the questions ahead of time
- Make sure you set enough time aside so you are not rushed (meet face to face if you can)
- Have them describe your strengths and weaknesses
- Ask them how they would describe you to others
- Ask them what they have learned from you life
- Have them describe what they think your calling is
- It is important to be open to what is said about you, and not to hold a grudge for criticism that you have asked for
- Ask people who know you well
- Remember they are providing nothing more than their point of view.

THE 8 PARTS OF A LIFE LIVED WITH PASSION

It is your turn to be the archeologist. Before you, in the pages of your notebook, are tons of clues about your life. You have written your hopes and dreams. You have brought to mind the stories of your life. You have looked at what brings you joy (and what steals it away). Now comes the time when you are going to mine all of this data about your life and start to make a plan for what you want your life to look like. The archeologist, as he sifts through the sands, appears to be looking for things. He is not looking for physical things—what he is looking for is the story of people's lives. He does not know the people who lived the stories, and he doesn't have written record. What he is reduced to, is finding small physical arti-facts. From these artifacts, he tries to piece together the story. He may look like a scientist (and archeologists are well-trained scientists), and he is using science to understand what each artifact is, but in the end he is not doing science. He is doing art. Just like a writer, he is telling story, but unlike the writer, who pulls the story from within, the archeologist tells the story by digging in the ground around him.

You too are going to have to be an artist. You are going to need to look past, the simple facts and ideas that are written down. You are going to need to look to the see the story they tell. Let's take one of my best friends, Joia, for example. She is a musician. One her favorite people to play and collaborate with is our buddy, Edwin. The two of them work really well together. They share common vision, but have gifts that complement each other. When they were working on a new song, time just seemed to fly by. While working the Five Million Dollar activity, Joia wrote down, "Pay Edwin's salary so he wouldn't have to move away." On the surface, it would be easy to deduce that Joia didn't want to lose her friend, but what is the story behind that hope? Obviously, one of reasons was Joia values Edwin's friendship. But the artifact also pointed to the fact that Joia also really enjoyed having a great collaborator in her life. The artifact had two stories behind it.

Up to this point, I have talked about living a life with passion. When I say this, I mean your soul longs not for one thing, but it longs for many things. It longs to be you, but "being you" is a complicated multifaceted creation. What our soul really longs for is a full, rich, balanced life. We might find one or two pieces that fill up much of our time and energy, such as our family or a job. No matter how large that piece is, there will still be a number of other areas of our life in which our soul longs for completion. What you are going to do now is mine all the activities you have completed to find the stories of what you want your life to look like. As you look through all that you have written, figure out what you would like your life to look like in eight different areas. These areas are spirituality, immediate family, friends and family, physical health, education, personal finance, work, and leisure. Make sure you come up with a vision for all eight areas.

The 8 Areas of Your Life

You are going to create a vision of what your perfect life would look like in all eight areas. Each of the eight areas is described in great detail below. In your notebook, write the name of each area on its own sheet of paper. Divide the piece of paper into three columns. In the right hand column, write all the dreams for that area of your life. Dream big! If you want an MBA, write it down. If someday you would like to own your own business, adopt children, see the world, give away one million dollars before you die, see your children married, write it down. Don't just write down the first things that come to mind, spend time thinking about each area of your life.

One of the best sources for information for this process, is all the work you have done to this point. Look back at all of the work you have done. Reread each section. Figure out why you wrote what you did. Mine those lists. Pay attention to how you feel as you read each item. Some will make your soul leap right inside your skin. Pay attention to how you feel as you read the list. Pay attention to the themes that appear over and over again. Take your time with this. Let it roll around in your head for a number of days. Keep refining your vision. Just like all art, there is no right answer to this. You are writing the story of your future, a life you can live with passion. In understanding that, this can be a daunting task. I have provided a little guidance for each of the eight sections to help you start framing your answers.

SPIRITUALITY When I do a similar exercise (which I will explain later), the title I use is "relationship with God and the Body of Christ." This certainly expresses a certain disposition that I have. Use the term that is most appropriate for your life. Here is where you would list what you would like your prayer/meditation life to look life. In terms of relationship to the Body of Christ, this is where I include the service that I try and do. I also have included my desire to be more thankful for what I have been given.

IMMEDIATE FAMILY This section should be devoted to relationship with spouse and children. Since you are painting a picture of what your perfect life would look like, include what you would like to have happen in the future. Having kids (or more kids) would be included here. Maybe you want to adopt. Or you are not married, but hope to be someday. Also, consider what you would like to pass on to your children. I am not talking about what you are going to leave them in your will, but what types of life lessons you want to pass on to your children. Do you want to teach them about honesty or faith?

FRIENDS AND FAMILY Would you like to spend more time with your parents (or less)? Do you feel like you don't have any close friends, but would like a few? Also, don't be afraid to mention specifics. Maybe you were lucky enough to grow up around your cousins, but your brothers and sisters are scattered all over the place. Maybe you will name that you would like to get together with all the cousins of your children's generation once a year. Is there someone you are mentoring (or would like to mentor)? Write that here.

PHYSICAL HEALTH When it comes to physical heath, oftentimes we only think of the things that we do (or in most cases *should* do). Also, consider things you would like to stop doing such as smoking and eating fast food.

EDUCATION I am a firm believer that we need to be learning at all points in our life. When we are learning, we are keeping our minds sharp. Also, as we continue to learn we are exposed to new and different ideas which change our view of the world (challenging the way we act) and change our view of ourselves (challenging what we want out of life). I believe that everyone should have a continuing education goal. This doesn't mean that you have to be working towards a degree. If you would like a degree, write it down. Consider the things you would like to learn. Dance the tango. Play the guitar. Bake really good bread, which I still long to do. These don't have to be skills that help you in your job, though they could be. What you should want to learn, are skills that improve the quality if your life.

PERSONAL FINANCE This section is going to come much more into focus when you are working through Part IV which is devoted completely to the topic. Not only write your goals about sending your kids to college, homes to buy, and retirement, but also include the money you would like to tithe. Be specific. List the percentage of your income you would like to give (not what you give now), or list a specific goal. I have a goal to give away three million dollars in my life and when I die, to have a trust set up with a million dollars in it to keep doing work long after I am gone. Am I every going to reach these goals? I have no idea, but I think it is worth it too try. (NOTE: Be careful here. Don't compare your life to mine or anyone else's. Write down what you want for your life.)

WORK/VOCATION Depending on where you are in your understanding of what you want your life to look like and who you are, this section is going to be the most varied from person to person. You might be in a situation in which there is a job out there that you know your soul is longing for, but you are not doing. If that is the case, you would write that here. Be careful not to limit yourself to just one thing. Other things to add to this section would be characteristics of the type of job you would like. Be home every night by six so you can have dinner with family. Have four weeks of vacation a year. A job that has a set salary and it not based on commission. Finally, include in this section characteristics of your self that are at your core. I would consider part of my vocation being a storyteller, therefore visions of my perfect life include becoming a better storyteller.

LEISURE Here you are going to include types of play that you would like to do. See where your grandparents migrated from. Swimming with the dolphins. Seeing puffins in the wild. These may not seem like noble pursuits, and you might even think they are a little selfish. A life filled of only these things would be shallow, but they are important.

THE PARTS OF PASSION
- On 8 sheets of paper in your notebook write one of each of the following headings on each of the pages: Spirituality, Immediate Family, Friends and Family, Physical Health, Education, Personal Finance, Work, and Leisure
- Divide each page into three columns.
- In the far right column, write the characteristic of a perfect life in that area. Write as many items as you would like, but you should try and have at least four or five on each page. (Examples: Personal Finance-be debt free, Immediate Family-go on a date with my wife one a week, Education-learn to play the guitar)

Note: *Nothing is too big or too small to write down. Don't be afraid to dream, but also do be afraid to be simple. It is okay to say that your perfect description of your immediate family, is to say evening prayers with your daughter every night. Some people are afraid to write something so "small" as evening prayers as part of their perfect life. That is part of the reason we spent so much time trying to name the things that bring you joy. Many of the things that bring us joy are so simple, and easy to call into our lives. Don't think in terms of magnitude. If it is part of your vision for a perfect life, write it down.*

Imperfect life

Just as important as it is to know what you would like your life to look like, I think it is as equally important to know what you don't what your life to look like. I don't think that you should dwell on, or fear, what horrors are awaiting around the corner, but there is value in knowing what you don't what your life to look like. Often times, we can find ourselves migrating to things that steals the life out of us. If we don't have them named, we are less like to avoid them. You are now going to go through the same eight lists and name what the worse case scenario is.

WORST CASE SCENARIO
- In the left hand column of the eight sheets of paper in your notebook, describe what the worst case scenario is in each aspect of your life.

Where are you?

Now you have determined what you would like your life to look like, and what you hope it will never become. At the beginning of the book, you made a brief, but honest, assessment of where you are in your life right now. Most of the questions then were about how you were feeling about the state of your life. Take a less emotional and more analytical look at your life. In each of the eight areas, figure out where you are in comparison to the two extremes. You are not being graded on this, so I don't want you to inflate where you are. If you are only half way there, don't say you are three quarters of the way there. It will do you no good. At the same time, don't beat yourself up. Just because you are dissatisfied with one part of your life, doesn't mean you rate it much closer to the worst case scenario than it deserves to be. Where you are right now is a fact of life. It is a statement of fact, nothing more. This is a tool to help assess what you are going to need to get where you want. Be honest and analyze, don't be overly optimistic or overly critical.

WHERE YOU ARE
- At the top of each of the pages in the center column, draw a line between the two outside columns.
- Place a 0 at the left end of the line, and a 10 at the right end of the line.
- Determine on a scale of 0 - 10 your life is in each of the eight areas. 0 being your worse case scenario and 10 being your perfect vision. Place an "X" on the line and give it a numeric value which represents the present state of your life in that area.

Rough Draft of the Rest of Your Life

You have just written a possible rough draft for the story of the rest of your life. You have created the best and worse case scenario of what your life can look like. You have also named where you are right now. The vision you now have is much more than most people have in their whole life. The most exciting part is you have just begun. As time passes, even greater possibilities for your life are going to unfold before you. Now, in the middle of this hope, a dose of reality. Just because you have named where you want to end up, doesn't mean the work is over. Not only is there work to be done, but there are also obstacles in your path which are keeping you form where you would like to get. Let's deal with those next.

HURDLES AND BARRIERS

Simply knowing what we want and getting it are two different things. There is no magic pixie dust we can sprinkle on our head and get what we want. There are hurdles and barriers between us and what we want.

Obstacles are things that keep us from our dreams. As I have said before, I have a number of learning disabilities. I have ADHD and a whole cocktail of reading and writing disabilities that are most easily described as dyslexia. Like I said, I have stopped using the term "disabilities" when I talk about what I deal with. I always use the term "obstacle" instead. Obstacles are something that exist—that make it harder for us to get to our destination. Disabilities are just what the word implies—things that disable us from doing something. The conditions I have in my life are obstacles that often times makes is harder for me to do something than the person next to me. It doesn't disable me from doing it. I might have to work harder, or differently, than those around me, but it doesn't stop me. Your success or failure depends on you, and how you choose to act. It doesn't matter if others have the same obstacles or not. The obstacles that exist in your life are there. You just can't wish them away. The best thing to do is to name them and deal with them.

We are going to spend sometime looking at the obstacles you face in your life reaching your dreams. It is important that you participate in these activities fully and not just read through them giving them a little thought. It is much easier to deal with an obstacle that is named, than to be surprised by trouble. That is not to say that we are going to name all of the obstacles you are going to face, but the more you name, the easier your task is going to be. By naming the obstacles, you are going to be able to attack them head on instead of reacting to them. It is important that you are honest with yourself. There is going to be some self assessment. If you gloss over your reality, then you are just wasting your time and not preparing yourself. I don't want you to be Chicken Little, screaming "The sky is falling!" Strike a balance in your assessment.

What is stopping me?

Make list of all of the obstacles you are facing in living a life with passion. It is important be honest, but don't make trouble up. These obstacles could be money, age, education, location, self esteem, support from others, or physical condition. Maybe you want to be a painter, but know you are going to get grief from your family because they think you need a *real job*. Maybe it will be hard because you are accustomed to a certain level of living, and to follow your dream will compromise that. You might feel too young or too old to follow your dream. List every possible obstacle you face right now. When you do this, look through two lenses. The first lens, is to list all of the obstacles in the short term. These are the obstacles that you are going to face as you get started, and the obstacles you will face to maintain. The second lens is worse-case-scenario obstacles you are going to face. No, I don't think nuclear war should make this list. If there is a nuclear war you are going to have much bigger problems than following your dream to finally get a college degree. But you mother dying might be an obstacle in the future. You could be in a situation where your mother is taking care of your aging father and you would then become responsible for his care. I don't want to sound heartless and cruel by having the world revolve around your needs, but it is important to understand what you face.

Take a look at each of your eight lists one at a time, come up with a list of everything that is stopping you. What are all of the obstacles that you face in living a life with passion. Consider everything. It is hard to admit that the reason you can't chase the job you really want is because you are afraid what your parents are going to say. That is a real obstacle in life. We think we are reasonable adult. We are not little children. There is no way we would let what our parents think stop us for doing what we long to, right? Wrong. It is shocking the number of

decisions we make in our lives to please other people, especially our family. The only real way to insure that you are going to be able to knock your obstacles down, is to name them. If you make a list that is incomplete, then you are going to make it much harder for you to reach your goals. I will admit that you are not going to know all the obstacles that the world is going to present, but the more obstacles that you name, the more likely you are going to reach your goals. Think of every possible reason for what is stopping you. Write every one of these obstacles down the center of the page between your worst and best case scenarios.

OBSTACLES
- Take each of the eight areas of your life one at a time, and come up with a list of every obstacle that is preventing you from having the life your soul longs for
- Consider every possible obstacle
- It is very important that you are honest with yourself in this exercise. The more obstacles you can plan to attack, the more likely you are going to achieve your goal

---

Your Problems vs. The World's Problems

I think it is useful to split your list of obstacles in to two categories: 1) the obstacles you create for yourself; 2) the obstacles the world creates for you. It is important because the way you face these two types of problems are different. Here are a few examples. You want to be a doctor, but you feel that because you don't have a medical degree, you can't start today. This would be an obstacle of the world. The world at large requires that you have a medical degree before you can open a practice. On the other hand, you want to be a writer and you feel that because you don't have a English degree, you can't start today. To be a writer, you don't have to have an English degree. There are lots of writers who don't have English degrees. This would be an obstacle of your own making, because it is a barrier you have given yourself. Now some of these obstacles are going to take some thought to categorize. For example, you might have listed not having enough money to pursue your dream. If you have sat down with the numbers, and realized that you are going to need to have thirty thousand dollars to buy all the equipment you need to start your small business, and you don't have the money, then that is a problem of the world. On the other hand, you are considering going back to school and you don't think you can afford it. Because you have not looked at the numbers or spoken with your family about the sacrifices they will have to make to help you, then that is an obstacle of your making.

Often times, the obstacles that you have created can be eliminated from your list with a little research. The obstacles we have created for ourselves are there because we are guessing that they are going to be obstacles. Go through this list and see which obstacles are just guesses. Do the research to see if they are real obstacles. Challenge your own assumptions. This is an easy way to eliminate obstacles that are not there. The ones that you don't eliminate, you will now have a better understanding on how to tackle the obstacle. For example, some friends of mine wanted to write a book about experience of losing a family member and what they learned in the process. It would have been easy to say there was no way to publish this book. They could have thought, "We are not writers. There is no way a big publishing house is going to pick us up. We could try self publishing, but it is too costly, and we know nothing about laying a book out, and getting an ISBN." With a little research, because of the wonders of modern technology, it is possible to do print on demand, which is nothing more than the ability to print books in quantities of 10 - 250, often at three to five dollars a book. That is not the same as getting books printed for a dollar each, but to get those prices you would need to print thousands of books. With a little research, they were able to find a way to share their experience with family and friends. Did they end up on the New York Times Best Seller list? No. Did they make millions of dollars? No. They gave most of the books away. But those weren't the goals. The goal was to share what they had learned in life with family and friends. A little research eliminated the obstacle of cost, because it was never truly an obstacle.

We don't like admitting we are wrong or failing. I know when I name self-imposed obstacles, I feel like I have failed. It might make you feel a little better in the short run to blame the situation (obstacles the world imposes), but if that is an inaccurate assessment, it is not going to help you in the long run. It is helpful on this step to get help from another set of eyes. Have someone you trust look at the list of obstacles. More than likely they will have a more objective view point on what is self-imposed and what is world-imposed.

TYPES OF OBSTACLES
- Go through all eight lists of obstacles, and classify each obstacle as either a self-imposed or a world-imposed obstacle
- Place an "S" next to the self-imposed and a "W" next to the world-imposed obstacles
- Group the obstacles in your notebook by type
- Review (maybe with someone else) all of the obstacles that have a "W" next to them. Reevaluate to see if it really is an obstacle of the world, or one that is self-imposed that you have projected onto the world
- Review all of the obstacles that have an "S" next to them. Determine if they really are obstacles. This may require research.

Ordering Your Obstacles

You have two lists of obstacles. Order them from "hardest to get around" to "easiest". I know this is guess work, but do the best you can. It will be easiest if you break them into four tiers of difficulty: "very easy", "easy", "hard", and "very hard". As you move forward with following your dreams, you are going to attack these obstacles from hardest to easiest. This might seem counter intuitive, but it is really not. In his book EAT THAT FROG, Brian Tracy uses the example the first thing you should do everyday is eat a frog. If you start your day by eating a frog, everything gets easier. To organize your work, you should do the biggest, hairiest, least enjoyable problem first. By doing this, you accomplish two things. First, you get the hard stuff out of the way so it can't get worse, but only get better. Second, we avoid the biggest problem each day, and then all of a sudden we are out of daylight and stop working. This pattern can continue. This way, the biggest problem never gets done.

ORGANIZING YOUR OBSTACLES
- Categorize each obstacle as "very easy", "easy", "hard", and "very hard"

Dealing with the obstacles

In my mind, the biggest challenge in dealing with obstacles, is naming them. Once they are named and brought out into the light, they seem much less menacing. Also, when we see the specific problems, they are much easier to tackle because they become manageable. We are smart people who can handle small problems. When we get in trouble, is when we see too much of the picture—we get overwhelmed. For example, if you and your friends decide to do a group trip to Italy and somehow you end up in charge of the trip. At first this can seem like a lot, but if you break the organization into parts it gets much easier. The things you are going to need to organize are travel to the country, travel around the country, housing, visa and passport questions, activities, and food. You know how to look for the cheapest flights. You know how to buy train tickets. You decide it is not your job to be Cruise Director Julie and everyone can choose their own activities. All you need to do is figure out the subway system in Rome. Instead of planning every meal, you decide to find one nice restaurant in each site for a big dinner out, but every other meal, everyone will be on their own. Now this is a lot of work, but each of the tasks are manageable. Living with passion is no different. You are a smart person and you can handle all the small stuff.

It is important to understand the difference of how to approach the two types of obstacles. The obstacles of the world are often the easiest to deal with. Getting past the obstacle may not be easy, but because it is something outside of ourselves we can look at more honestly and see the path past it. The obstacles we create for ourselves are much different. Because they are part of who we are, the path past them is not as clear. For example, if you are held back because you are concerned what your parents are going to think. There are some many factors at play here. You want to live the life you want, but you understand how much they have given you. They want what is best for you, but have a very narrow definition of what that "best for you" is. Ultimately, you going to need to do what makes you happy, but sometimes that is harder than it sounds. If you are looking for a specific strategy for attacking a particular obstacle, I highly recommend Stephen Pollan's book SECOND ACTS. Stephen does a wonderful job in naming 12 different categories of obstacles and specifically how to deal with each type.

ACTION PLANNING

You are starting to understand what it is you want your life to look like. It is now time to start to craft a plan. Once you have a plan, it will be much easier to start the financial planning part because you will have an understanding of what you are really trying to achieve. I cannot stress enough how important having clear goals can be. At the end of this section, I share my own experience with written goals and how I deal with written goals daily. In Brian Tracy's book THE 100 ABSOLUTELY UNBREAKABLE LAWS OF BUSINESS SUCCESS, he contends that if you take out a piece of paper and write down ten goals in the present tense, such as "I weigh 180 pounds," and place that piece of paper in the drawer of your desk.

When you come back a year later 8 of the 10 will be accomplished. Sound unrealistic? After I read that, I was skeptical. So I made my list of 10 things I wanted to accomplish. Instead of putting them in a drawer, I hung my list on the wall above my desk. I didn't look at the list every day, but every now and then it caught my eye. Three weeks later, seven of the ten things on the list were either done or scientifically underway. Goals work. The example of Chris I used in the intro was a simple demonstration of goals in action.

Creating goals

The steps to creating goals are very easy. First, you need to decide what you want. Up to this point, that is what we have been talking about. By naming the experiences you want in your life and experiences you don't want, you are more likely to move towards them.

Second, write your goals down and be as specific and clear as possible. An idea that is written down, is a goal. An idea floating around your head is nothing more than a fantasy. I know in my life when there are things that I really need to get done, I will tell a few friends, creating a bit of an accountability structure. I have heard myself say something, making it more real. They have heard me say something, so my word is at stake. It is more likely to get done. Also, by writing an idea down it will help crystallize what the goal actually is. For example, take this book. The idea was kicking around in my head for over three years. I even spoke on the topic a number of times all over the US. Even with me, speaking on the topic was just vague sense of "I want to write this book." Then one day I stopped fooling around. I realized that this was a book I needed to write, it was information that I thought I should share. I wrote a goal on the dry erase board in my office. I simply wrote, "1000 words every day." After three days, I modified the goal. I added the word "twice". It has worked. Some days I was just not feel-ing it. It would have been easy to think that the book was really a large project that was going to take a great deal of time. *If I miss one day, no big deal. Right?* Wrong! On days I felt I didn't have any ideas I wrote anyway, because I knew I was making progress. By having a specific goal it gave me something to shoot for. It was no longer something large, write a book, but it was something I could do today. The smaller goal of writing 1,000 words a day, clarified for me the amount of effort I needed to put forth each day to reach my bigger goal of writing a book..

Third, you should set deadlines for each goal. A time frame gives your goal some urgency. I love travel. I was built to wander. One of the goals I have in my leisure section of my goal list is visit 40 countries by the age of 40. The goal gets more specific, "A visit is constituted by spending at least 6 days in the country." This is to prevent the 10 countries in 14 days trip in Europe. I am sure that is a lovely vacation, but can you say you have seen France if you have seen the Eiffel Tower and had lunch in the train station. I digress. If my goal list said 40 countries, I'm sure I would do more international traveling than most, but I have my whole life, which is very long. It will happen eventually. I made this goal when I was 28 years old and at that point I had "visited", in my definition, 6 countries. Doing the quick math to reach my goal I have to visit three countries a year. Is that realistic? Probably not, but it has given me some urgency. Each year when I buy my next wall calendar, I look to see where our natural breaks from traveling for work are. I then write the places I might visit during that time. Because of the deadline, I am getting to two or three countries a year

Your goal list

Now you may not realize this, but you have basically done most of the work on a goal list. In creating what you would like your life to look like in each of the eight areas, you have named where you are and where you would like to be. These are your goals, but they are not written as goal statements yet. More than likely you have three or four goals for each area of your life. Assuming you have three in each section, you have twenty four goals. That might seem a little much to manage, because it is. You'll be surprised once you get started, how quickly you will start knocking them off the list as completed. It will take work, but you can do it.

When I was kid I use to play Dungeons & Dragons with the neighbors. Before we could start playing, we had to create characters. Each character had six main characteristics, such as strength and wisdom. At the beginning of the game, each of the characteristics had a value in the range of three to eighteen. The values were generated by rolling three dice. The three numbers were added up to give value. Each player got to choose after the roll, which characteristic the value would be added to. If you wanted to be a wizard you would put your highest value for wisdom, which was needed to cast spells and your lowest on strength because you would engage in little hand-to-hand combat. You had six sets of rolls and you needed to decide how you were going to use those values.

Your life is no different. Right now you have eight different values ranging from zero to ten in the different areas of your life. You have a limited amount of time, talent, and treasure. You are going to need to choose which goals you are going to apply what you have to offer. In order to do this, narrow your goals down to ten goals. This will be much more manageable to start. Once you have chosen the ten goals you are going to start moving towards, you are going to write each of them in the present tense, as if you have already accomplished them. Make sure you include a deadline. For example, if you want to get a college degree in Education you will write, "I have a Bachelors of Arts in Education in the Spring of next year"

Now this is where it is going to get a little funky. You are going to need to trust me on this. Twice a day, once in the morning and once at night, read your ten goals out loud. Read them with the energy they deserve. They deserve lots of energy because this is what your soul wants. As you read them, imagine what it feels like to have them come true. As you read, "I am debt free on January 1st!" What does that feel like? Feel all the stress of living paycheck to paycheck evaporate. Feel what it is like to have the phone ring, and to pick it up without worrying it is a collection agency on the other end of the line. Read the line with passion and feel the success of living the goal. This may seem like a lot of psychological hooey. I am not going to bore you with self-efficacy studies that show how this really does work. If you want to know that, knock yourself out with a little research. I do know this, it works.

Remember back in the section on prayer I told you about my friend Jason, who prayed for an end to hunger, then started feeding people. He understands the power of seeing hunger being ended, because he sees it in his own life. Because he has a clear vision of it happening, it is easy for him to act in the right way. If you state over and over (as well as feel over and over) what your future is suppose to be, you will start moving towards it. If you are trying to get out of debt and you spend time (just for a few moments) feeling what it is like to have no debt, how easy is it going to be for you to meet some friends at the mall for lunch and not walk out with a new outfit? It will be very easy because you are living in your vision of the future what your soul wants.

Do it everyday! If you think this is crazy, wait until you see how I use a goal list.

CREATE A GOAL LIST
- Choose the ten most pressing goals for your life from the eight sheets
- On a new sheet of paper in your notebook write out each goal in the present tense as if they are already completed, with a deadline.
- Twice a day read the goal list out loud with passion. Envision what it feels like to have each of these goals completed.

How You Know You Have Achieved Your Goal

You will never be perfect. Even if you achieve your vision of a perfect life, you will want more, for you will see even more possibilities. I was on a flight recently and overheard three flight attendants chatting before takeoff. One said to the other, "If I die today, it will be okay. I will have done everything I wanted to do in this life." Since I have a tendency to butt into conversations of which I am not really a part, I suggested that she make a new list. Her first reaction was a puzzled expression, but then she smiled. Before we landed, she showed me the beginnings of a new list of things she wanted to accomplish in her life. That said, it is important to have targets to shoot for—goals to strive for. It is equally important to know whether or not you have hit your target. By knowing what success looks like, you will be able to tell if you are heading towards your goal. You will be able to determine whether or not you are really living out this vision of life. In most cases, you are going to use the vision characteristics from the eight aspects sheets. If I look at my Physical Health sheet, one way to tell if I am achieving the physical health I desire, would be to observe that I now weigh 180 pounds. To be able to tell if we are living up to the goal, the goal itself needs to be measurable. Now, in this case, it is very easy to measure if we have achieved the 180 pounds; however, if the goal is to have a better relationship with your daughter, you're going to have a hard time measuring your level of success. For these situations, you are going to need to use Soft Side Values.

Soft Side Values

In the world of business, there are many ways to judge success. How much money did we make? How much did each product cost to produce? What is the value of our stock? There are formulas that can be created to measure outcomes. These formulas are called metrics. If we are using a metric that creates a solid value, that value would be referred to as a Hard Value. Metrics can be useful in our daily lives as well. Many people who are trying to lose weight, keep a weekly or daily record of exactly how much weight they have gained or lost. Diabetics track their blood sugar level daily. We look over the last year to see how much money we've saved each month for a down payment on a house. Though you may never have referred to them as such, these are all metrics that produce a Hard Value.

Metrics are a way to measure, but they have their limitations. School systems encounter these limitations constantly. How are they supposed to measure how much a child has learned? Sure, they can create an exam that tests the child's knowledge of facts and which types of problems he or she can solve, but to what extent does that really measure how much they know?

As you go through this process, you are starting to name the person you would like to be. But how do you measure the extent to which you are being a better parent? How do you measure whether or not you are growing closer to your spouse? There is no scale that you can climb onto that can measure love. There is no formula to see how close you are coming to your dreams. So how do you do it? The answer is Soft Side Values.

The first place I encountered the term "soft side values" was in a column written by Marshall Goldsmith in September 2003 issue of FAST COMPANY. He talked about the same idea—about how to use metrics in our daily life. The concept of soft side values is not used to measure outcome (since in these cases, it would be impossible), but rather a measurement of steps that need to be taken. The term "soft" is used because we are not dealing with hard facts, such as finance. For example, one of your goals could be that you want to be a bigger part of your son's life. Everyday when you come home from work, before you do anything else, you find your son and spend 15 minutes with him. You ask him about his day, you play with his toys, you are present. The goal is not to spend 15 minutes with your son, but to be more present in his life. You may not be able to measure presence, but you *can* measure time. Spending that time with him every day, doesn't necessarily equate to you being more a part of his life, but it is a step that can help that process. It is also something you can measure. You have taken something that can't be measured and created a way to at least measure your effort, helping you to reach your goal.

MEASURING YOUR GOAL
- For each of your goals write a statement (or statements) that demonstrate what it would look like for you to achieve each goal.

Your Declaration of Independence

This may sound like the corniest idea you have ever heard. Your friends may make fun of you if you do it; however, make no mistake, it works. This is nothing more than another creative way to work with your goal list: make it into a piece of art.

Take your goal list and ask a friend who is an artist (or has really good handwriting) to write your goals up on some fancy-schmancy piece of paper. You can get really cool, "artsy" paper at any art supply story for a few bucks a sheet.

Have everyone in the family sign it. Buy a nice frame and put your goals in it. Hang the goals in the living room. Not only will it be an interesting conversation piece, it will be a constant reminder of what you want your life to look like. It works just like the goal list I carry in my pocket. Every time you walk past it, read it. Do it out loud. I am not joking. Sure, you will feel like a doofus, but just tell yourself one more time what you want to be. Perhaps you will be on the way to crash in front of the TV, and instead will get motivated to go work towards a goal.

Every single one of us knows what the Declaration of Independence looks like. It is nothing more than simple words with a few signatures after it, yet it is a powerful document. It is the hope, the dreams of a country. This is your Declaration of Independence. This is your declaration of freedom from a day-to-day lifestyle, embracing instead a life of value and joy. Sign it. Date it. Think about what it will be like to show it to your grandchildren. The record of the day you decided what you wanted to become.

More than likely, if you are thinking that this is a stupid idea, it is because you are afraid to put your dreams out to the world. It is one thing to hold your dreams in your heart, but another to tell the world. You could fail. They might see you as a failure. They might think that you are foolish. You need to get over that fear. If it is something you want, you must be willing to fight for it, because it won't always be easy. If you desire something, you must get past what others think. This is about your life, not theirs. Take control of it.

How I Use a Goal List

I am going to share with you how I use a goal list. You may think that I go overboard. I am not going to contest that fact, yet I can tell you this: once I started using the process, it changed my life. There are now weeks in which I get more done than I had in three or four months in the past. This is not an overstatement for effect; it is the truth. Even if you don't go to the extent that I have, stating goals will change the way you live your life.

Every morning, the first thing I do is to get out my goal list and to recopy the entire list. I have found that by taking the time to write out all the goals again, I make it impossible to just skim over them, which I might be prone to do if I was simply re-reading them. I then reread the list three times throughout the day. I read them before lunch, before dinner, and right before I go to bed. I told you I go overboard. I chose these times because I know that I am going to do all three of those things each day. It has helped me to create a routine with my goal list. If I said that I was going to read the list three times a day, most days I would end up reading the list three times at bedtime. Days have the tendency to slip away like that. Relating the re-reading with daily activities, gives me a little more structure.

Now, I am going to show you how to really go overboard. My goal list is broken up into seven different categories from the eight we talked about (I don't have an immediate family section since I haven't got one). Under each category are two sections, side-by-side. The column on the left is the "big picture" ideas about the goal. The column on the right is the specific goal I am trying to accomplish at the moment. My seven sections are as follows:

DEEPEN MY RELATIONSHIP WITH GOD AND THE BODY OF CHRIST This is the first goal because, in my mind, it is the most important. This section reminds me to take time to pray, to be thankful for what I have, and to be in service of others. Big Picture category examples: be thankful, spend time in prayer, serve those in harm's way. Specific category examples: go to daily mass, give thanks for 10 things each day, night prayer.

GAIN, NURTURE, AND MAINTAIN RELATIONSHIPS I am a deeply driven person when it comes to the work that I do. I always throw myself headlong into whatever project I am working on. Many times, this is detrimental to the relationships I have. This is my reminder to make sure that I care for those relationships. Secondly, it is a reminder of how important it is to add new people to my life. New people challenge our world view and help us to grow. Finally, in this section, I have a list of people who are chasing dreams right now, dreams for which I have a skill to help. It is a daily reminder to ask, "How can I help Mike today?" Big Picture: find old friends, support others. Specific: Paul, Joia, Mike.

PERSONAL HEATH This is pretty self-explanatory. We need to steward the gift that is our body. I know that the healthier I am, the better I feel. The better I feel, the more confidence I have and the more willing I am to chase my dreams. I don't think we take our personal heath serious enough. Sure, we are in a hyper-conscious, image-based society, but we tend to only think of health in terms of how we look and when we are going to die. I believe that it is a much bigger issue that just that. For me, it is a real stewardship issue. Our bodies are one more gift that we have been given. Just like it is important that we care for how we use our money, we need to care for our bodies in the same way. You only have one body. I believe I need to do all I can to care for mine. Big picture: eat better, work out. Specific: never eat out alone, don't eat fast food, stretch everyday, run and climb every day I am not on the road.

LIFE-LONG LEARNING I think we should always be learning something new. It keeps the mind sharp and makes us more well-rounded as people. It also opens us to new opportunities and dreams. Big Picture: business, Spanish, theology. Specific:

30 minutes of non-fiction reading a day, only listen to books on tape when driving in car alone.

VOCATION This is the traditional sense of the word vocation. This is about the work I do and the work I would like to do. It is the goals around getting better at the work I do now, and a reminder of the types of work I would like to do in both the near and far future. Big Picture: be a better story teller, tell more stories. Specific: blog daily, see one movie a week.

FINANCIAL STABILITY Again, self-explanatory. You will have a much better idea of what this should look like after reading part two of this book. Big picture: be debt free, invest justly. Specific: invest $300 a month, donate $300 a month, donate three million dollars in my lifetime.

PLAY This is my list of all the really cool things I want to do before I die. This section only has one column at this point in time. Big Picture/Specific: 40 countries in 40 years, be a horseman, live in the Far East for nine months.

After I rewrite these seven areas, I write 10 large, specific goals in the present tense as if I have already completed them. Examples of goals I have or have had in the past: I own a hybrid car in December of 2005 for which is paid for in cash. I am debt free February 28, 2004. I improve the quality of Jerry's family's life by selling 500 copies of his book SONGS OF HOPE in the two weeks after it went to press.

If your first thought is that there is no way you can get all your personal learning things done each day, much less goal in all seven areas, you are right. Most days, if I do a good job, I will do one or two things from each section, but having my goals (what I want to be) in front of me four times a day, reminds me who I want to be and how to craft my life. If I remind myself four times a day that I would like to have a certain level of health, I am much less likely to buy the candy bar I don't need at the gas station. If one of your goals is to spend time daily reading to your daughter, you are much less likely to get caught up in something at work, and more likely to get home on time.

It is amazing the way your life will be transformed when you confront your dreams four times a day (or just once a day or once a week). You will spend much less time playing solitaire on your computer or watching mindless TV, because you know there are things you really want to do and a person you really want to become. I believe that goals are so important that I am willing to make a bet and I am not a betting man. I believe that if you take the goals system I just laid out, and use it faithfully for one month, you will be more productive than you have been at any point in your life. If this is not true I will refund the price you paid for this book. Just send me a note at gene@monterastelli.com and I will send you a check. It is a win-win for you. Your life will improve or you get your money back.

You Need to Start

All the planning in the world is not going to do you any good, unless you do something about it. That may seem obvious, but this is where most people fall down. In order to change your life, you need to change your habits. The reason our lives look the way they do, is because of the habits we have, the things that we do everyday without thinking. You have already taken the steps of naming what your life is like now, and naming where you would like to be. That was very important work, but this is the most important step. It is time to start. This is the reason that I look at my goal list every day. I know how easy it is to slip back into my old ways. I know that even after having worked at this for a long time, I still need to work at it every day. By looking at my goal list every day, I re-explain to myself what I truly believe is important. Again, as I stated in the beginning, you will not be able to change your habits by simply deciding to do so (or at least mere mortals like myself won't). Making those changes becomes easier when we keep re-understanding our motivation. Those who become successful are not because they have learned a formula that works in their lives. They are successful at their chosen definition of success because they implement that formula every day.

Do something every day to get yourself closer to your goals, even if it is just one small action. Every action you take, puts you one step closer to your goal than you were before. Most of the goals we will seek in life are too big to achieve in one day. Realistically, most things worth doing are not accomplished in one day. You will also find, each time you take a step forward, it helps to build a little momentum. Think about trying to push a car that is in neutral. At first you push and push and push, but feel you are making no progress. As time passes the car moves a little, and then it moves a little more. With each passing moment the car starts to move a little faster and a little faster, until it feels like the car is moving itself and you are just walking along with it. The same thing will happen as you start moving towards your goals. At first it will feel like you have no traction and are not getting anywhere, but as time passes you will start moving faster and faster until it feels like your goal is actually coming to you. When I worked as a computer consultant, one of my managers would say, "The first fifty percent takes fifty percent of the time and the second fifty percent takes ten percent of the time." He was not an English major who couldn't do math. He simply understood momentum. The only way you can take advantage of the power of momentum is to start, and start today.

It might be helpful to have specific goal or outcome for each day. In the example of writing this book, instead of stating I was going to write everyday, I gave myself a number of words I had to write each day. Each day I made myself sit down and write one thousand words in the morning, and one thousand words in the evening. There were a number of days that I would feel like I was done writing. I would then highlight the section and do a word count: 540 words. Ouch. So I would press on. I would admit in some of these forced writing sessions that the work wasn't my best (and in some places it was just really bad), but it kept me moving forward. It would get me thinking about how I wanted to present a particular topic. Sometimes forcing myself to write bad stuff, helped me to understand how I didn't want to explain a topic. When the section was rewritten, it was much better.

It is possible that you don't know where to start or what to do first. Not knowing what to do is one of the main deterrents we face in life. It doesn't matter if you know what you are doing, you need start. Do what you think you are supposed to do first. It will probably be wrong, but you will learn what the right thing is. You are just exerting the first few pushes on the car you need to move. Don't be afraid to ask for help. No matter what you are trying to do, someone has tried to do something similar in the past. The simple fact is you need to begin now. As was once famously said, "Like the sand through the hour glass...these are the days of our lives." Look at your goal list. What are you going to do today to get that momentum started?

Getting Help

One thing that is very important about following your dream is to remember you are not to do it alone. I'm not sure what it is about human nature that makes us so willing to help others, but refuse to ask for help. I'm sure it has something to do with the fact that we don't like to look helpless. If we are helpless then we don't have value. We have it so skewed and backwards. We can see the importance of helping others so clearly, but it's so difficult to ask for it ourselves. We need to get over ourselves and ask for help.

There are parts of following our dream that we are not very good at. For example, you might feel very compelled to start a small business. You will have lots of passion for the product you are producing, but don't have the first idea of how to start and run a business, and I have a feeling you won't have a passion for tax law. For every aspect of your dream that you are not good at and don't have passion for, there is someone in the world who does or will be willing to do the task for a fee. Get out your list of obstacles. Next to every obstacle, write the names of people who you can go to for help with each one. Some obstacles you may be able to handle on your own, but many won't be worth the time it would require you to handle them. Ask for help. The worst thing someone can say is "no".

Courage in Making a Plan

I received a very exciting phone call from one of my favorite people in the world. She called to tell me she has the opportunity to doing something she has dreamed about for a very long time. It is a life-changing opportunity, and with all life-changing opportunities there is a lot to consider. She asked me how I am able to take risks in my life to follow the nontraditional path in my own life. So I told her:

First, I am a dumb hick from Wyoming who doesn't know any better. There have been many times in my life when, once a situation was over, I realized that I had been in much greater danger than I thought at the time. I am generally oblivious, but because of that I am not debilitated by fear. As my father always says, "A little fear is good." A lot of fear makes it impossible to act. Disconnect from your fear when you have to consider a choice. Ask the question, "What would I do if I had no fear?"

Second, it's all a big game. If I truly believe the profession of faith that I proclaim, then I know how the story ends. This life is placed in context for what it is, a short amount of time in the context of eternity. Even if I didn't believe that after this life I would spend eternity with the Supernatural, life is a long trail. Many times we fret and fuss over situations that, in the long run, seem much less significant. It is easier to make a choice when you don't think the world (or your world) depends on it—because in most cases, it doesn't.

Third, I am looking for the right struggle, not the right solution. There is nothing that makes me happier in the world than the pursuit of dreams. Choosing something to believe, or what to become, and giving what I can to achieve it, lights me up. It is amazing the obstacles you can overcome when you are possessed by a dream. You find in yourself courage and ability you didn't know was there. It is not that you find courage and ability to do everything, but just enough to face the challenge, task, or step that is before you now—leading you closer to the dream. Just enough to get you to the next step. At the next step you somehow find more, more in yourself and more in your world. The outcome is not what's important, but the passion that you pursue it with, and the growth that happens along the way. A choice is easier when success is judged by who you are and what you learn, not if you achieved the original vision. Many times you will realize as you grow closer that the original vision is flawed and you find your way to something completely new.

That's Not Very Spontaneous

Right now you might be thinking, "Wait a minute. We are chasing dreams here. What is the deal with all these lists, and goals? This seems like a lot of planning. Shouldn't dreams be more spontaneous?" I think being organized gets a bad wrap. Again, full disclosure. I am ADHD. I can't stay focused long enough to pick up the socks in my room without being distracted by something else. When I clean up my room I have to say over and over again, "Pick up socks. Pick up socks," or I will get distracted. I was even on Ritalin (a.k.a. vitamin R) for 18 months and stopped taking it because it is a personality-altering drug and it was killing my spontaneity. I love the work I do partly because it provides the flexibility on a moment's notice to drive up to Philadelphia to have dinner with a friend, because I am my own boss. I love spontaneity, but I still think organization gets a bad wrap.

What is more amazing, is the number of places that being unorganized is tolerated as part of the culture. "I am on youth ministry time." "Oh, you know how those artist types are." It is amazing and it has got to stop. Now I am not saying that you need to become anal retentive, but this is out of control. Richard Leider and David Shapiro, in their book WHISTLE WHILE YOU WORK, suggest (and I think rightly) that the reason we love people who do things spontaneously, is that it seems almost divinely appointed. "Oh look what they were able to pull off with almost no effort." It is as if we believe God wanted it that way, while those who plan and prepare must being doing something that is really not part of their nature.

I also think we love the rush of adrenaline. Doing the work at the last minute—facing the deadline. It is a challenge and we have survived. It gives us stories to tell of how we were able to succeed by working right up to the end. Really, how sexy of a story is it to say, "The reason we succeeded is because we developed a carefully structured plan. We met all of our milestones in a timely fashion. We were done with time to spare." Who wants to tell that story?

It has to stop now. When it comes to reaching your dreams, live an un-sexy, planned approach. You are thinking, "Where is the fun in that?" The fun is *living* your dream. The more organized you are about approaching your dream, the more fully you are going to live your vision. There are lots of broken dreams along the roadside of life. They are not broken because the person chasing the dream wasn't talented enough to reach their dream, but because they didn't work efficiently toward their dream. I know this sounds horribly dry and boring. Let's take your finances for example. You will see in the next part of the book, the keys to financial success are discipline and a little education. You can't fix your financial future in one sitting, but you will see it requires that for months you take a few simple steps to insure your long term health. Following a budget is boring, and very un-sexy. But not losing sleep over the future, and knowing that you get to provide for your family and your family's dreams is amazing.

It is not possible for me to be that organized. It is not in my nature. It may not be your natural tendency, but you can learn to do it. The question is not, "Do I want to be organized?" The question is, "Do I want to live my dreams?" If the answer is "yes", then you owe it to yourself and your family to work the best you can. At the end of your life if you have chased a dream and failed, you will not regret not getting to the dream, you will regret all the things you could have done better.

Dabble

Going through a process like this can be very exciting and educational. It can help you to find a purpose in your life. At the same time, it can also be very frustrating. In a little bit, we will deal with many of the pitfalls of the process of trying to find and live purpose in your life. But let's look at one right now. To this point you have done all the exercises faithfully. All your work is in one neat clean notebook, and you still have no idea what you are to do with your life. You are not alone. For some people as they go through this process, the future lays neatly out before them. For others that is not the case. If you are in this situation, I have a simple suggestion for you: dabble. Treat the experiences of life like a giant buffet. When I go to a buffet I have never been to before, I sample lots of things to see what I really want to eat. To this point, you have named lots of experiences you know you enjoy (at least a little). Give them a try in small doses. Really, this is good advice for anyone who is trying something new.

For example you might, through this process, uncover the fact that you have always wanted to be a painter. But being a painter can mean lots of things. It could mean a job, a hobby, or the kitchen in off-white. Just because you think you want to be a painter, doesn't mean that you should quit your job, spend thousands of dollars on supplies, and sign up as a fulltime student at an art school. More than likely, the better course of action is to take an inexpensive non-credit community college class. In the end you might discover that you didn't really want to be a painter, but you just wanted an excuse to wear a beret.

Not only will trying lots of new things give you a better understanding of what activities you enjoy, but it will also expose you to a whole new community of people. A few years ago I decided it would be fun to learn to play a musical instrument. I have played lots of instruments for a short period of time. I figured I was older and a bit more mature. Maybe now I would have the discipline to practice like I should. So after some investigation I chose the concertina. The concertina is a little squeeze box, much like a little accordion without the piano keys. I also figured it would be fun to take lessons. Even living in Washington, DC, I couldn't pick up the phone book and get an instructor. So I did some research. I found out that one of the best concertina players in the world, Noel Hill, did a couple week-long camps in the US. The price was right, so with concertina in hand, I headed out to Oregon for music camp. By no means am I now a professional. Only very rarely does the concertina make its way out onto stage with me. Trying the concertina, I ended up with an experience I never would have imagined possible. I spent a week in the woods of Oregon, at a retreat center where all the meals were homemade, with the wackiest group of people I had ever met in my life. All very good people, but definitely wacky. They were there because they loved playing this very unique music. There was a fulltime poet, a guy who could play anything on bagpipes, and a guy who could sing iterally hundreds of sea shanties. One of my classmates recorded everything on a reel-to-reel tape deck (opposed to my mini-disk player). One person spent years making dulcimers. When the folk revolution ended, he started running the foundry that did all the bronze work of his wife's sculptures, and the there was a good Christian family man who traded me his magic tricks for my juggling skills. It was such a cool week. An experience I never would have found if I hadn't asked, "What would it be like to try the wacky little squeeze box?"

You are not going to figure out what your soul is longing for with a bunch of exercises and a notebook. The questions I have been leading you through, will help you bring clarity and get you to ask yourself some questions you haven't asked in years. But when the rubber meets the road, you are going to need to experiment with your life. As you try something new, ask yourself, "Would I like to do this again, regularly, for the next week, or the rest of my life?" It is okay to say, "It was good that I did that once. I don't need to do it again." If nothing else, you have had a new experience and crossed one more thing off of your life's list. Always keep in mind, life is the sum total of everything you do. By seeking, you are seeking what you want to add to your life, not the one thing your life is going to be.

WORK

We spend most of our waking hours working. For many of us, we even work more hours a week than we sleep. Also, it can't be denied that the work we do provides the income we need to take care of our material needs. Because of this, there are two special notes I would like you to consider when it comes to choosing the work you do, while living your life with passion.

You Don't Have to Love the Work You Do

I need to make one thing abundantly clear: doing work that you love does not equate to living the life that you love. It is possible to have a job that you don't "absolutely love" and still have the life you want to live. It is also equally possible to have the job of your dreams, but still be nowhere near the life you want to live. I love my work—so much so that I lay awake at night longing to do my work—but that is not going to be the case for everyone. To be honest, because I love my work so much, there are a number of places in my personal life that have suffered because I have been so driven by my work. When I am not on the road speaking, I work from home. There are times in which I can get so consumed with a project that I can go literally days without looking up from my computer. No matter what your work is, there must be balance. I have had a great example of balance in my life: my father. He is living the life he wants. What is more remarkable is that he does work that he doesn't necessarily enjoy.

There is no one I admire more than my parents. The lives they have witnessed to me by their actions color much of what I am today. No one has taught me more about work, and the balance of work and life, than my father. My father is a very bright man, with an amazing memory. He graduated from Northwestern University with a degree in engineering. He loves good food and the theater. He really enjoys big cities. So how did he choose to live his life as an insurance salesman in Casper, Wyoming? The job he does, he does well, but I'm sure it isn't the most intellectually simulating. I'm sure he would prefer to be in a big city with its culture. Why is he living the life he has? Because what is important, is the sum total of his life. Because of his fixable schedule, the only time growing up that my father missed something I was in, was because one of my siblings was doing something at the same time. My father worked a job that afforded us a wonderful quality of living and the ability to send his kids to whatever college they chose. Sure, he goes into work most mornings before 5 AM, but he can leave at 3 PM to go officiate a high school soccer game. My father would never use the word "ministry" to describe his involvement in high school sports. But there is not a soccer player in the state of Wyoming in the last 15 years who doesn't know who my father is, and they understand he thinks they are important and loves being a part of their lives. Because he works for himself, he can take time off to travel with my mother (or the whole family). My father's job is not who he is. It is nothing more than a tool which allows him to live the life he wants.

Pasquale Vignochi

My grandfather, Geno, was a tough old man. He was a first-generation American. As a child during the depression, he helped feed his family by shooting pigeons with his BB gun. As an adult, he ran a bar in a small mining town in western Illinois. The mine ran three shifts. When you get off work after a long day you want to get a burger and beverage, even if you worked third shift and got off work at 8 AM. For this reason, the bar was open 16 to 20 hours a day. So my grandfather not only worked long hours, he also worked very hard hours.

My grandfather had a business partner by the name of Pasquale Vignochi . (The bar's name was "Gene and Pasquale's".) He was quite a character, and as the stories go, he was bootlegger during the prohibition. Pasquale lived a hard life. He left home at 13 because of his hard home life. Pasquale was able to find work in a cobbler shop. In addition to giving Pasquale work, the family he worked for also helped take care of him. I have a feeling that at age 13, when his peers were going to school and playing soccer in the streets, he would have liked to join them. But, he didn't have that choice. He was fighting for his life, literally. It was not a question of what he wanted to do in the moment. It was about the life he wanted to live. In order to get to a place where he could live the life he wanted, he had to make sacrifices in the now.

This struggle is going to come up over and over in the course of this book and the course of your life. The question is what is more valuable to me, my desire for "in the moment," or my desire for my life? I am not contending that you are going to have to delay fun and happiness all the time. But it is important to always understand what your goal is, the life you truly want to live. How would you act if you where fighting for your life? For Pasquale, because he was basically living on his own at 13, he had to make choices that kids didn't have to make. This is about your life, not those around you. It is not a matter of what's fair. It is simply about your situation right now and where you would like to be.

I would encourage you, when you get to a point where you are not sure if life is treating you fairly, and you don't have the strength to make the choice that is best for your life—think of Pasquale. Think of the sacrifices that the generation before you made, to give yourself the opportunity to struggle with this question.

PITFALLS

With each task, we try and complete there are obstacles. You have already spent time with the obstacles you face in living your life with passion. Most of these obstacles are very specific to the task at hand, or the situation you are in. For example, you might need more education for a specific job. Or, there is great pressure for you to stay near the family in Maryland, when you feel called to live in Arizona. Both of these examples are specific to you and your circumstance. In addition to obstacles that you will encounter specifically, there are also other troubles to be aware of. In my life of dream chasing, I have encountered a number of pitfall that are not specific, but can be found in a number situations. You will not encounter all of them, but you will bump into some. If you are aware of them as they approach, you are much less likely to fall into their clutches. Here are some of the pitfalls of living a life with passion.

Beer Commercial Cool

One trap that needs to be avoided (or at least that we need to be wary of) is the trap of looking to create a life of really cool experiences. It is very easy when creating any list of goals in our lives, to create a list of all we want to do, but what we are trying to achieve here is creating the people we want to be, not just the things that we want to do. I know that my prose is littered with stories from my trips around the world. A friend of mine was recently giving me a hard time for starting a sentence with phrase, "I was sitting in this small cafe in Ecuador..." I cherish the memories I have crafted. These experiences provide really cool dinner party stories, but they are not who I am. My life must be much more that a bunch of super cool beer commercial moments. *You know it really doesn't get any better than this!* Life must be a narrative. It must be a story. The reason we like a story is because the characters change, they grow, they become new people. How boring would a story be if the character didn't change? Our lives can be no different. We must grow and change.

Now I am not discounting these moments either. I know I learned a lot from my trip to Ireland (the one where I became an accidental tourist), or the time I decided to strip my life down, sell everything I owned, and live out of a car for 18 months. Those were events that have given me some great stories, but what is more important is the perspective I gained. Those moments forced me to change and grow.

"Everyone thinks their wife is beautiful and their child is smart." The reason that statement is true is because a husband gets to see his wife every day. He get to see how extraordinary his wife is by living next to her, day to day, in the simple moments of life. When her compassion is shown for a stranger. When she cares for her own father. When she gives of herself to the cause she believes in. She is beautiful. The reason that statement is true is because a mother sees her daughter everyday. First, she is this unformed little blob that can't even keep her own head up. Then she opens her eyes. She recognizes people. She says words. She knows where the cookies are kept. She is a little sponge, learning at warp speed. You know she is smart—you can see her learning, almost effortlessly, on her own.

That is the narrative of life. The day to day, as we become the people we want to be. Oftentimes we seem to stall in our life. We stop being challenged. Each day looks like the next. Wake, shower, breakfast, work, lunch, work, dinner, watch TV, sleep. Somehow our life seems to lose the fact that it is a narrative. We become a story that no one wants to read. One of my favorite TV shows of all time is KING OF THE HILL. It is the story of a normal family living just north of Dallas. The father, Hank, sells propane and propane accessories. The mother, Peggy, is a substitute teacher, which she knows, not believes, is a very high calling. There are two kids at home. One, Luanne, is a niece who has nowhere else to turn. The other is Hank and Peggy's son, Bobby. They don't travel much, except maybe to the Boggle state championship. They get up and go to work everyday. It is a great show, because it is about daily life. They are constantly challenged by their friends and family to state who they are, by the lives they live.

Standing on the glacier on the top of the highest active volcano in the world, Cotopaxi, will give you perspective on your life. Sometimes it will only give you a great picture to put in the Christmas letter. For me, I am sure the experience is closer to the latter than the former. Was it a bad experience to have? No. It was beautiful, and a fun day spent on the other side of the world with fellow travelers I may never see again. Am I a much better person because of the experience? Probably not.

As you make this quest to become the person you want to be, make sure you are using the right metric to judge the process and your life. It is easy to be jealous of those around you who tell cool stories, but your life is more. You should judge your life on whom you are becoming, not the stamps in your passport.

Golden Handcuffs

The second pitfall that you need to be aware of can be called "The Golden Handcuffs." The term was introduced to me the summer between my junior and senior years of college. I took an internship working for a large insurance company in a mid-sized mid-American city, the population of the metro area was 100,000 and close to 200,000 in the surrounding area. I was a systems analyst intern. Basically, it was my first chance to use my newly minted computer science skills in a "real world environment." I was no longer doing assignments at school, which were framed as real problems. Instead, I was working alongside people trying to create an application thwy were going to use in the field. Not only did the project have to work in the budget and time we had, but it also had to really do what we said it would. It was great education, as internships should be, not just about computer science and business, but of life.

The reason I say it was more than an academic exercise about my field and business is because of the people I was surrounded by. They were all good people. And the adjective "good" does them no justice. They worked, not only hard, but well. They were committed to each other as a team and their families at home. One of the conversations we had over the course of that summer was about the fact that everyone took more than the half hour lunch they were given. Really, that extra 15 minutes wasn't harming anyone, right? In the end, the group decided they were being paid to chat and that wasn't fair to our employer. From that day on, lunch was 30 minutes, like it was supposed to be.

Life was good in this sleepy mid-American town. The schools were good, the streets were clean, and there weren't the visible social ills—but it wasn't Chicago. Sure, life was nice, but you couldn't, at a moment's notice, decide to go to a play. Good Vietnamese food was impossible to come by, though you could get burritos as big as your head. Other than one showing as part of the cinema club on the university campus, there were no art house films to be found. Not that any of these are needed to live a good life, but it was enjoyable to have those options. Chicago was just up the road, but really it couldn't have been further away.

One day at lunch, Joe explained to me why the move to Chicago was impossible for most of them. Cost of living was much less in their town, so to maintain the same standard of living they would have to get a major pay increase. Second, if they wanted to send their children to the same quality of schools, they would either 1) have to live out in the suburbs (adding a long commute, instead of the ten minutes we all had), or 2) sending their children to private school (which would add strain to the budget). Their life was good, but they found themselves locked in golden handcuffs. Sure it would be great to live someplace more exciting, but life is good here. To them is wasn't worth risking good to try and get great.

It is an easy trap to fall into. To believe that our lives are good enough. Please, be very clear, I am not in any way disparaging their lives for the choices they made. I use their situation because Joe used his own life to, in some small way, warn me while I had freedom to choose a life I truly wanted. Not to settle. We always have that choice in reality, but the consequences of our choices are different at different points in our lives.

They are very happy. One of my roommates that summer, after graduation, took a job with the company we worked for. He is now a homeowner and a father. He umpires baseball and volunteers at a local tax advice center to help those who don't know how to fill out their tax forms. He is in a loving marriage and very active in his church. He has carved out the life he wants for his family and himself. It is just as important to ask yourself, "Am I living the life I want, or am I settling for good enough?"

Disposition vs. Location

One of my favorite Taoist stories...

ONE DAY A STONECUTTER WAS OUT WORKING AT THE FOOT OF A MOUNTAIN, CUTTING OUT LARGE PIECES OF MARBLE. AS HE WAS WORKING, HE HEARD A COMMOTION. HE LOOKED UP THE ROAD AND SAW A PROCESSION COMING HIS WAY. IT WAS THE KING. IT WAS LAW THAT MEMBERS OF THE KINGDOM BOW AS THE KING PASSES. THE STONECUTTER STOPPED HIS WORK, TURNED TO THE ROAD AND BOWED. AS HE WAS WAITING FOR THE PROCESSION TO PASS HE THOUGHT TO HIMSELF, "HOW WONDERFUL IT WOULD BE TO HAVE THE POWER OF THE KING WITH EVERYONE HAVING TO BOW TO YOU." ALL OF A SUDDEN THE STONECUTTER WAS THE KING.

HE DIDN'T QUESTION WHY HE WAS NOW THE KING, BECAUSE HE WAS ENJOYING HAVING ALL THE PEOPLE BOW TO HIM. AS HE RODE ON TOP OF HIS HORSE HE WAS REALLY ENJOYING ALL THE ATTENTION. AS THE DAY PASSED HE GOT HOTTER AND HOTTER, FOR IT WAS A VERY SUNNY DAY. HE ASKED FOR A HAT FROM ONE OF HIS ATTENDANTS. AS HE WAS PUTTING THE HAT ON, HE THOUGHT, "HOW WONDERFUL IT WOULD BE TO BE THE SUN, FOR THE SUN'S POWER IS SO GREAT EVEN A KING MUST HIDE FROM ITS HEAT." ALL OF A SUDDEN THE STONECUTTER WAS NOW THE SUN.

AS THE SUN, HE WAS ENJOYING HIMSELF. HE WAS SO POWERFUL HE WAS MAKING CROPS GROW AND PEOPLE HID FROM HIS HEAT. ALL OF A SUDDEN A CLOUD WAS BLOCKING HIM. HE THOUGHT, "HOW POWERFUL A CLOUD IS! HE CAN BLOCK THE MIGHTY RAYS OF THE SUN. I WISH I HAD THAT MUCH POWER." ALL OF A SUDDEN THE STONECUTTER WAS THE CLOUD.

AS THE STONECUTTER WAS ENJOYING BEING A CLOUD AND BLOCKING THE MIGHTY SUN, HE STARTED TO MOVE. HE REALIZED HE WAS BEING MOVED BY THE WIND. HE THOUGHT, "HOW POWERFUL THE WIND IS! IT CAN MOVE THE CLOUDS. I WISH I HAD THAT KIND OF POWER." ALL OFF A SUDDEN THE STONECUTTER WAS THE WIND.

THE STONECUTTER LOVED BEING THE WIND. HE COULD GO ANYWHERE HE PLEASED. SOMETIMES HE WAS THE GENTLE BREEZE THAT SPREAD THE SEED OF PLANTS AND OTHER TIMES HE WAS A MIGHTY WIND THAT POUNDED HOMES. THEN HE HIT

THE MOUNTAIN. NO MATTER HOW HARD HE BLEW, HE COULD NOT MOVE THE MOUNTAIN. HE THOUGHT TO HIMSELF, "HOW POWERFUL THE MOUNTAIN IS, IT CAN STOP THE WIND. I WISH I HAD THAT KIND OF POWER." SUDDENLY HE WAS THE MOUNTAIN.

AS THE MOUNTAIN, HE WAS SO LARGE THAT PEOPLE WOULD LOOK TO HIM FOR NAVIGATION. THEY WOULD CHANGE THEIR TRAVEL PLANS TO GET AROUND HIM. HE WAS RELISHING HOW POWERFUL HE WAS. THEN HE FELT SOMETHING. HE FELT HIM-SELF GETTING SMALLER AND SMALLER. NO LARGE CHUNKS AT A TIME WERE BEING REMOVED, BUT HE COULD FEEL HIS POWER SLIPPING AWAY AS PIECES OF HIM WERE BEING CHIPPED OFF. HE LOOKED DOWN AND SAW A STONECUTTER.

The third pitfall to watch out for is change for change's sake, or mistaking what part of your life needs to be changed. To this point, we have shined a very bright light on our life, maybe a brighter light than you have shined on it in a very long time. This can be exhilarating as we find new opportunities, but it can also be horrifying as we find decay and atrophy. Our first thought is, "I now have a much clearer vision of my life. I need to change this and this and this and I will find joy." It is easy, in the moment, to get invigorated, but this is not about making change on the surface, but at the core of who we are. Many times that change is not a change in what we do, where we live, or who we spend our time with, but it is a change in our disposition.

This book is not a manifesto calling you to quit your job and follow the passion in your soul to work in the rainforest of the Amazon. Some of us will be called to this. Most of us will continue where we are. Sometimes what needs to be changed is nothing more than our disposition. Maybe all we need is to understand that our life is really much better than we thought. There is so much we should be thankful for in our everyday lives, but miss. For many, in the begin-ning, it is nothing more than a change of priorities. You change the way you manage your money, so you lose a great amount of stress from your life. With this simple, though not necessarily easy, change you now have a new disposition in life—you find joy where you are. Or after a great deal of self-examination you change the priorities in your life. You keep the same job, but instead of coming home from work and plopping down on the couch, you head down to the community center and teach English as a second language. You have not changed location, but have changed your disposition—how you face life.

The Toothpick Maker

You might be the greatest toothpick maker in the world. Not only can you produce them faster than others, you do it with a craftsmanship that astounds the masses. You are flown all over the world to make toothpicks for world leaders. Those who long to make toothpicks make a pilgrimage to your shop to learn from you—the master. Does all of this add up to knowing that toothpick-making is your vocation? Maybe, but maybe not.

Finding your vocation is not the same thing as determining what you are good at. Sure, it is a helpful part of the process to know what your talents are—and many times that will lead us to joy—but that doesn't mean that is what our soul longs to be. Also, knowing what you are good at may lead you to an occupation that "pays the bills," while you pursue your passion in your free time. If your giftedness equaled your vocation, then finding your calling would be as easy as taking a standardized test. Just fill in the ovals, run it through the computer, and you have your vocation. But it is not so.

Sure, there are those prodigies, like Mozart, who start composing at five. He was a man who was haunted and consumed by music. He had so much music in his head, he spent his whole life trying to get it out. That is just not most of us. A great old movie, RAISING BOBBY FISHER, deals just with this subject. The movie is about a boy who is a chess prodigy. The struggle of the child's parents is what to do with his amazing gift. At one point the father says, "He is better at this than I will be at anything in my life." The struggle becomes not how to use the gift, but to find balance in the kid's life. Something Mozart was not capable of doing.

Sometimes. many times, what's much more important than talent is passion. History has shown, many great writers were not good in school or had learning disabilities. They were told over and over they should give up on writing and get a job in manual labor. In the end, it becomes their struggle to follow their passion that shapes their work, and more importantly the people they become. A keen understanding of what we can do is important, but it is not equivalent to a keen understanding of who we long to be.

Here Comes the Clown

For eighteen months of my life, I basically lived out of my car. I sold everything that I owned and drove from speaking engagement to speaking engagement. Whenever I made it back to the Washington, DC area, which was basically home, I would crash with the same friend each time. He even gave me a key to his place so I could just show up when I needed to. About a year into my journey, my friend moved from a condo in the suburbs to a beautifully restored row house in a historic neighborhood in the city. To say the very least, I was jealous. When I was growing up in Wyoming, this was the home of my dreams. A beautiful row home in an up-and-coming neighborhood. It was just too much.

A few months after my friend had moved into his new home I showed up, unannounced as always, to find he was hosting a small dinner party. The table was set beautifully with wonderful food the host had made. Around the dinner table were three couples, all about my age with a one-year-old running amuck. There were four lawyers, a teacher, and a woman who was just about to finish her physical therapy degree. Of the three couples, two were homeowners. Then I came ablating in, disheveled from the road. Immediately room was made for me at the table and I had full plate of food in front of me.

As I came in, I felt mortified. Here I was walking into what I have always dreamed adulthood should be. Cool home, good conversation, great wine, beautiful spouse, real jobs, and here comes the clown. The one guy who hadn't managed to grow up. Instead of owning a home, I had everything I owned in the car parked out front. Instead of having a real job, I was what I am. Sitting down at the table, I felt like a little kid. I felt like I belonged in the hallway eating dinner off an ironing board, not at that grown-up table. Then everything changed. One of my friends asked me what the next little bit of my life looked like. Without hesitation I said, "Friday, I fly to Iceland for a week of horseback riding with my mother. I am back in DC for three days. Then I am off to Ecuador for a month to study Spanish." In that moment, not only was I happy that I didn't have a home, or a grown-up job, I could feel the eyes of longing and jealousy from the dinner party guests as they all thought of getting up tomorrow to go to their "day job."

When you live an unconventional life, there are times that you are going to feel like a fool and a clown. This isn't the only moment in my life that I have been surrounded by other adults where I felt like I was filtering my life away. On the other hand, there have been times in life when I was afraid to talk about what was going on in my life. Not because I was embarrassed about what I was doing, but because it was so rich and wonderful. I feel embarrassed because I am living my dreams, and those around me aren't. There are going to be moments where you believe the grass is always greener on the other side. It is human to feel that way because you only see a small part of the other side. You have to focus on what's right for you. Life is not some one-size-fits-all American dream. Focus on getting where you want to go.

Not Knowing

Most often, once people are this far along in the process they are refilled with energy. They feel like their life is starting to be given back to them. They feel like they are, for the first time in years, heading in the right direction. This may not be the case for you. Instead of having a direction (or a re-affirmed old direction), you are more confused than when we started. Maybe, as you were trying to create a goal list, other than learning how to bake really good bread, you can't come up with anything else. That is okay. You should not feel inadequate because you are now trying to find your vocation, but somehow have ended up more lost. I have felt that way for years of my life at a time.

What is the next step if you just haven't figured the big picture out? I turn to Eastern wisdom and the often-quoted fortune cookie, "The journey of a thousand miles begins with one step." The important thing to do is to start moving. You might remember from high school physics the term "inertia". Basically, inertia can be simply summarized as "objects at rest have a tendency to stay at rest and objects in motion have tendency to stay in motion". For example, think how hard it is to push a car that has stalled out. At first, it is really hard to get the car moving (especially if you still have the emergency brake on), but once it gets rolling, it gets easier and easier to move. At a certain point, it starts to feel like the car is moving itself. That's inertia in action. Our lives are the same way. Getting started is the hardest part, but once we get moving it is easy. When I started working out daily, it was really hard to break up my daily routine to, in the middle of the day, stop what I was doing, change clothes, drive to the gym, work out, come home, shower, and then continue my work. After about a week, it became part of my routine and was easy.

Even if you don't know, big picture, where you want to head, start moving. Start making simple steps in your life. Take a class at the local college in something you are interested in. Learn to play the guitar. Take a cooking class. Volunteer at the local grade school. Find something that you might enjoy and do it. Oftentimes we feel we have to know where we are heading before we move. It is like the conundrum we give high school seniors. All they have known in their whole lives is school, and we are asking them to choose a major for the work they want to do. Some of them have a very clear idea what they want to study, but most don't. Even if you know what you want, it doesn't mean that won't change. Look at me, for example. I knew I was going be a computer scientist. Loved the course work. I lasted in the field for one year before moving on to something else. It is okay at this point to have an undeclared major in life. Start taking the introductory classes; you don't need a major till your junior year anyway. Just start moving.

Passion vs. Fad

For much of the past three years of my life, I have been without a major dream, an all-consuming passion. That is not to say that you must have one all-consuming passion, but for me it is a way I feel most comfortable. When Brad and I started our current ministry, it was that—an all-consuming passion. But that has changed. Not that I don't still have a passion for the work we are doing. I love it very much and it still feeds me, but today the work is very different than when we started. When we began, we had to figure out what our giftedness was, and how that fit into the world. After we did that, we had to convince the ministry world that it was possible that these two punk kids could use comedy, drama, juggling, and personal stories to first—hold people's attention, and then to share what we felt called in our hearts to share our faith. In addition to the traveling and performing, there were the entrepreneurial aspects of the work. We were creating a business and trying to convince the marketplace, and ourselves, that we did a viable form of ministry. After four years, much of that went away. We had a good idea how to run a business; how to explain what we did; and had done enough good work that we were getting enough work to live on by word of mouth. In a lot of ways the creation of the ministry was done. That is not to say that we did everything perfectly, and we knew everything. We were to a point of refinement, not creation. I still love what we do, and at no point soon can I imagine leaving this work, but it does not feed me in the same way, because the work I am doing is different than it was in 1996 when we started.

So there was this part of my being that was no longer being used. A part of my personality just sitting there. A part of my soul longing to work. As I said, for about three years of my life, I couldn't find that thing that would light me up. Now a number of times I thought I had found the next thing in my life. I would spend money on researching the idea. I would take classes. I would talk about the idea insensately with my friends. Then, six months later, it was gone. For some reason, the drive and passion were gone. This happened time and time again. I started to get very frustrated with myself. Where had my drive and follow-through gone?

So I sat down trying to figure out what was going on. I made a list of all the passions that had come and gone and the reasons I felt passionate about them. I also did the same thing for the starting of our ministry. I was amazed. The list of reasons were exactly the same with one exception. The ministry had lots of reasons for my passion (travel, speaking, creating a business, marketing, training adults, working with students who love God, working with adults who love youth), but all the new passions that came and went only had one or two reasons. I came to the realization that the new passions did excite my personality or light up my soul, but they only lit up part of my personality. Finally, one January morning I found this book. It became my passion. Not only did I love the subject matter, but also I loved working on the graphic design of the book and ads. I loved the marketing. I loved the fact that there were two very different topics to write on: money (analytical) and dreams (feeling). I was also getting more chances to speak, train, travel, and share and hear stories.

The reason I share this is not to illustrate how you should find one thing that feeds you in lots of way. That may happen to you. It may not. It has nothing to do with successfully defining and following your dreams. You might have one passion that feeds you in lots of ways, or lots of passions that feed you in one or two ways. Life is going to be constructed differently for every person in the world. The point is this instead: when finding the passions in our lives, we are going to encounter passions and we are going to encounter fads. Fads are just what the name implies. They are something that lights you up for a very short time, but passes as quickly as it came. That is okay. It is normal to find something you think is your passion, but it doesn't feed you in the way you would like. Don't feel like you have to stick with something when it is no longer feeding you. It is fine to move on. That doesn't mean you've failed. I have found that most folks in their lives are trying to find the place they fit perfectly. So they sit and think their mind knows the direction they are to go, then go there. My approach has been that there are millions of things in the world I could do. Instead of trying to find the perfect one before I act, I find one that I think might be right and try it. If it works out I stay with it, but more often than not, it isn't quite right. So I cross it off the list of millions of possible passions for me, see what I have learned from the experience, and try again. Chasing a fad does not mean you have failed. It is not a wasted experience as long as you learn from it and get up and try again.

Remember to Feed Yourself

One of the favorite parts of my life is the amount of time I spend with youth ministers. Most of them work too hard, for way too little payment and recognition. They do it because they love those they serve and the work they do. Youth ministers are notorious givers. All you have to do is ask, and they will try and give it. Even when they don't have it, they will try to find a way to get it. They are beautiful people who I am constantly inspired by. They try and take care of everyone who crosses their path.

The problem is that they are generally not very good at taking care of themselves. They are so selfless they can get themselves in trouble. The last time they were home before 10 pm from the church was the night the power went out. The last time they hung out with friends was when they left town to go to a wedding. The last time they went on retreat, they ran it. This is not uncommon for those who are following a passion that burns in their soul. I know I have been the perpetrator of these types of lifestyle choices at more than one point in my life.

I hated college. However,, I loved the learning. I loved the people I was around. I loved all the new experiences that I was having. What I hated, in my mind, was the decadence of my life. I was shutting everything down in my life to indulge in gaining knowledge. I felt very complacent. I wasn't doing anything. The way I compensated for that my junior year of school, was to be run a homeless ministry with over four hundred volunteers and be a resident assistant in a freshman resident hall. Oh yeah, at the same time I was working for the athletic department for work study, and taking more than a full course load of course work. About six weeks into the second semester, I got very sick. I was so sleep deprived I was down to 145 pounds, which is not where a six foot tall man belongs. I was taking care of everything and everyone around me. I was not taking care of myself.

For some reason, when we do something for ourselves, we feel selfish. There is great irony here. We will waste time with all sorts of silliness, but still won't take the time to care for ourselves. When I was senior in high school, I can remember hearing the story of a Japanese exchange student who had starved to death. He was so concerned about the price of food, that all he would eat was ramen noodles. He didn't die of malnourishment, he had enough to eat. He died of malnutrition. He didn't have the right types of food. He was so concerned about those around him, he didn't take care of himself.

This is common for those who have a passion of any sort, especially when it concerns caring for something or someone outside of ourselves. It is a dangerous pitfall to not take care of ourselves. I know in my own life, I have had to just get over myself. Get over my pride—of thinking I don't need (or deserve) to take care of myself. Get over my savior complex—thinking it is my job to take care of everything, and if I don't, it won't get done. A sick doctor does her patients little good. Not only is she less capable of helping her patients, it is possible she is going to get them sick. One of the greatest pitfalls of following your passion is only seeing what you are chasing; not realizing the vehicle (your body, mind and spirit) needs care as well.

I have found in my own life, I need to do more than just realize that I need to take care of myself. Since it is not my initial inclination, I have had to build in self-care to my daily life. As I plan my week, I make sure there is time for my physical heath. I make sure I am being challenged in my beliefs. Most important-ly, I make time to spend time in prayer, just listening. Every night before I go to bed, I go on a 20-minute retreat. I do a few minutes of thought-provoking reading and then I pray. Mostly I just listen. I try and listen to the day I just lived, I try and listen to my soul, and I try and listen to God. I have learned if I am not taking care of myself, I won't be healthy enough to chase my passions.

PART IV

Get Your Financial House in Order

You have a comprehensive plan for what you want your life to look like. Okay, so it isn't a comprehensive plan yet, but you're on your way. The next step is to create a *home* for these dreams to live and grow. There is no escaping the fact we live in the material world. We need housing, food, and transportation. We live within a system which requires money and financial planning. Our dreams are housed in the material world. Caring for that home impacts the way our dreams grow and to what degree we will get to live them. In creating a life you can live with passion, you need more than passion. You need balance with the world around you. For this reason, you also need a financial plan which will support your ability to live with passion. More than likely, your financial house is in need of a little work (or major reconstruction). You can do just that with a number of small steps.

NOTE: Through out this section, we are going to use the analogy of a rainstorm and a house when speaking of your finances. You might not have a lot of experience with personal finances, but you do have the experience trying to get out of the rain and of living in a house. We will use a house because, like a house, your finances are to provide you with protection and comfort. Houses require repair (your financial situation now) and maintenance (your situation in the future). Like all analogies, it is going to be an incomplete analogy. It is not going to work perfectly in all cases. In the end, it is nothing more than a tool to help us talk about the state of your finances right now, and what you can do to move forward.

Small Steps

I decided after a lot of prayer that I needed to place myself on the live kidney donor list. While deciding if I wanted to participate, I did a considerable amount of research, a good idea when you are giving up an organ! As I did my research two facts surprised me. First, the recovery time for the donor is longer than that of the recipient. Second, the better shape you are in, the faster you will recover. As committed as I was to becoming a part of the program I also understood the nature of the work I do. As part of a performing group, all of the work we do is a one shot deal. We speak at events that only happen once a year. I can't really call in sick. I understood that if I was going to have surgery, which was going to be scheduled when there was a need, I needed to be in the best shape possible so I could get back to work ASAP.

One of my greatest joys is rock climbing. I love it because it is much more than physical activity, it is a mental puzzle. Every time you go up a piece of rock, you need to figure out the most efficient way up. Also, it is an activity that clears your mind, because when you are 55 feet up, hanging on by three fingers, holding on is all you can think about. I try to climb at a rock gym every day that I'm not on the road. When it came time to get on the donor list, I had to give up climbing. Not because climbing and being on the donor list were incompatible, but I understood that I needed to get in to better shape. The climbing was good for me, but I didn't have time in my day to climb and do cardiovascular work. I still went to the gym every day, even more religiously than before, but instead of climbing, I would run on the elliptic runner. At first I was only able to run for 20 minutes with a resistance of level five. As time passed, and as I got in better shape, not only did the amount of time increase, but so did the amount of resistance. Because of the hard work I was putting in, I was getting in better and better shape. As time passed, I came to an interesting realization: once I had gotten into shape, it was much easier to stay in shape. If I missed a day or two, it wasn't that big of a deal. I was no longer trying to get into shape. I was merely having to stay in shape. In the beginning, the process wasn't easy. There were lots of days that I didn't want to drive 20 minutes to the gym only to abuse my body. Also, the elliptic runner was placed in the gym so as I ran I had to look at everyone having a good time, doing what I really love, climbing. But once I put in the hard work, once I had gotten into shape, it became much easier. I didn't have to run every day to stay in shape. It freed me up, once again, to do what I really loved, to climb.*

* As of the printing of this book I had not been the exact match for a person in need. If you would like more information on becoming a live donor, contact your local hospital or do a search on line for the terms "live donor" plus your state.

In the first half of this book, you began to name a life you can live with passion. Is that worth sacrificing for? Of course it is. And, much like getting physically fit, once you're in shape, it is much easier to stay in shape. The steps you take to get into physical shape, or financial shape, are not complicated. They do take discipline, time, and sacrifice. As you begin to create a financial plan that helps you to live a life with passion, it will be challenging. Just like getting in physical shape, you may have to give up some things you like to do for awhile, even while you jealously watch other people doing what you love to do. As daunting as this task may seem, consider the alternative—not ever achieving your dreams. In this section of the book we'll use simple steps to create a financial plan to move you toward a life you can live with passion. The basic steps:

- create a short-term emergency fund
- create a budget
- eliminate debt
- create a long-term emergency fund
- plan for retirement

Along the way we'll deal with questions about your spending habits, when and whether to buy a home, sending your kids to college, and charitable donations. Each step will build on the one before, so work through the steps in order. Move through each step carefully and thoroughly. This is not a race, it's the process that will allow you to craft the life you want.

If You Are Married

If you are married, you know there are very few issues as volatile as money. Money carries a lot of baggage with it. Issues of security, power, and future. There is no one way to approach money. People have a tendency to approach money with different attitudes. The situation can get more complicated if only one member of the couple is working or if only one person is doing the family budgeting and paying the bills. It is imperative that both people are on the same page regarding money. This is not an issue on which you can agree to disagree. You *must* have a shared vision of debt, savings, and spending. Am I suggesting that you sit down together to balance the checkbook? Yes! You *both* need to agree and understand your budget. You *both* need to know how well you are sticking to the budget. You must be in agreement on every major purchase and have a shared vision on minor purchases. You must agree on whether or not you will use money from the emergency fund, which we will talk about later. If you are not on the same page, you will not only *not* achieve your goals but this conflict will take its toll on your relationship.

If You Are Single

If you are single and you skipped the last section because you didn't think it wasn't for you, go back and re-read it. You might get married some day (at least your mother hopes so). Getting married is not just about being in love. It's about finding someone who you are going to spend the rest of your time on this Earth with, carving out a life together. This monumental (if joyful) task requires a great deal of communication and compromise. If you do decide to get married someday, there are important questions to ask each other. You need to understand each other's career goals, where you would like to live, and if you would like to have children. You must talk about money, sooner, rather than later. Not only do you both need to be educated about money matters and need to talk about how you will manage your finances as a couple, you also should know where each of you is starting from financially. Long before your wedding day, you need to know how much debt (and for what), the other person is carrying. I am not telling you that you should not marry someone because they have too much debt. What I am saying is you need to know what you're facing as a couple so you can plan for your future together.

I have heard people say they are not comfortable talking about money with their fiancé. But why would you get married to someone you can't talk about difficult issues with? These are not questions you ask on the first date, but you *must* talk about money. When people feel out of control, they feel stressed. When people feel stressed, they fight. Most people feel out of control about money because it points to issues of security and value. There is nothing couples fight about more. And the more problems you solve now, the less stress there will be later.

Did I mention you should talk about money?

THE RAINY DAY FUND

Picture yourself standing in the middle of a torrential rain, one of those rain storms where you're instantly soaked to the bone. The rain drops are so large you can feel each one hitting you. The rain is so heavy that you can't even see where you're going. Before you can consider what you'd like to do next, you need to get out of the rain and get dry. Does this sound like your financial situation? Feeling lost, overwhelmed, not knowing where to turn, and just looking for a place where you can rest to get your bearings. If you're standing in the rain, the first thing you need to do is get an umbrella, to create a little shelter so you can survey the situation. This will give you a chance to at least take a breath for a moment so you can look over the landscape to see where you are. Grandma always said you should have a rainy day fund. We'll call it an emergency fund. Your emergency fund will prevent unexpected problems from derailing your financial progress.

Creating a Short Term Emergency Fund

Emergencies will come up. It's a fact of life. You need to be prepared. You need to have a plan. You need to know what to do when all of a sudden you have a surprise bill. Contrary to the popular American ideal, the way you respond is NOT to get out the credit card. There are a number of reasons for this. We will talk about credit cards in great detail later. For now, just trust me on the credit card issue. Instead, you will use your emergency fund. What? You don't have an emergency fund? You will soon.

As you begin to get your financial life in order, you must prepare for an emergency at the same time you're working to get out of debt. The way you'll maintain that balance is by creating a temporary fund in the short term, go after your debt, and then create your long term emergency fund. You will first create this *short term* emergency fund of $1000. If you make less than $20,000 a year, your emergency fund can be $500. If you are trying to make a dent in your debt, but have to stop to cover an emergency, you'll feel like you're losing momentum. By having an emergency fund, it will insure that as emergencies come up you will deal with them without sabotaging your efforts to eliminate debt.

This money in your short term fund should be liquid. Liquid means the money should be easy to get to, not tied up in CD's, mutual funds, stock, gold, or Beanie Babies®. It should be easy to get to, but not so easy that you are tempted to use it for non-emergencies. The best option is to start a separate savings account that is NOT attached to a checking account for overdraft protection. The reason it should not be attached is because this money is to be used for emergency only. The fact that you didn't balance your check book and you bounced a check, does not count as an emergency. This account doesn't need a large return in interest. We'll talk at great length later about investing, but this is not an investment account. It is okay if it is earning only a few percent in a savings account.

I worked with a couple recently who had over twenty-five thousand dollars in debt. When we started, they began to work on their emergency fund right away. In the first month they were able to build a fund of $1000 without touching any of their regular income. They sold furniture on eBay that had been sitting around the house just collecting dust. They sold books and cd's on half.com. The wife was able to get a speaking engagement at a local high school. They also built a plan to get out of debt in 20 months. Even though the plan would require a lot of discipline and sacrifice, they were feeling good. They were on their way to financial freedom.

Then it happened, some sort of black fluid in the radiator. Bam! $400! The car got fixed and they started fighting to get the emergency fund back to $1000. Two months later, car number two needed work on the transmission. Another $500! They hadn't gotten the emergency fund back to $1000 when the second car needed work. Both cars were fixed, but the emergency fund was only at $300. They were frustrated to have both cars have problems at the same time. They were more frustrated that they had killed the emergency fund they had worked so hard to build. BUT, and this is a big but, they were able to take care of both cars without making any changes to their debt-elimination plan. They didn't have to give something up that was in the budget, to take care of the car. As frustrating as it was to use the emergency fund, it would have been so much worse to add more debt. Their next step was to get the emergency fund back up to $1000.

Commit to building your emergency fund right now! No matter what you have to do (legally) to get it.

- Look around your house at all the junk, I mean wonderful stuff you no longer use, that hasn't been touched in years. Sell it on eBay, half.com, Yahoo auctions, or at a garage sale.
- Could you get a second job?
- Search the Internet for opportunities to be mystery shopper. You can make as much as $50 for test driving a car and filling out some paper work.
- Save money that you normally spend, we'll talk more about some areas for potential saving later

This small step, like all the steps in this book, requires you to be committed to your goals (in this case financial stability). You must believe in the goals and you must act in a decisive fashion to reach those goals. Your money situation won't improve overnight. It will take hard work. Are you going to feel little stupid having a garage sale? You might. Which would you rather feel, stupid selling your kids old toys, or frustrated at not having $500 to fix your car? You may need to get creative. There is no Fairy Godmother out there who is going to wave her wand and make your problems go away. Only you can help yourself. It is better to start now. In a perfect world, you would be able to put this fund together in the next thirty days. Big task? Yes! Possible? Yes! You would be amazed at what you can accomplish when you put your mind to it. Might the process take three or four months? Yes. Don't be afraid to set an ambitious goal. If you don't get it done in one month, keep after it. You can do this. I know you can. You have no idea what emergencies are waiting around the corner for you. Find a way to do it. What are you waiting for? Do it. NOW!

What is a Financial Emergency?

Birthdays are not emergencies. A sale at Pottery Barn is not an emergency. Your parents coming into town unexpectedly and you want to take them out to a nice dinner is not an emergency. Regular maintenance on your car or house are not emergencies, those should be built into your budgeting. An emergency is the transmission dropping in your car. An emergency is the water heater dying in January. An emergency is an unforeseeable immediate need.

Before you take money out of your emergency fund, you need to take time in thought and prayer. If you are married, both you and your spouse must agree to use the money. Once you dip into the money, you should put your financial planning back on hold until you have rebuilt the fund.

ELIMINATING DEBT

To extend the analogy of the rainstore and the house...With your umbrella, you have managed to create a little bit of comfort and you have made it into the house. But there is a problem; there are leaks everywhere. These leaks are debt and foolish spending. Before you can worry about what is next, you need to take care of all these nagging leaks. Eliminating leaks is a process.

- Step One: Commit to adding no new debt to your life (with the possible exception of a home loan).
- Step Two: Calculate exactly how much debt you have.
- Step Three: Calculate where your money is going and find wasteful spending you can eliminate.
- Step Four: Create a monthly budget.
- Step Five: Live the budget.

None of these steps will be hard. Does it sound like a lot of math? Well, maybe, but it is only going to be adding and subtracting. The reason I have broken this process into 5 easy steps, is because it is so important. Living by a budget is the bedrock foundation to your financial future.   Only after you do these things, are you going to be able to move forward towards your other financial goals, such as retirement, paying for your kid's college, and buying a home.

Step 1: Never Add Debt Again

If you want to buy something, I have a great plan for you—it's called saving. Do I sound like an old fogey when I say that? Good, because our grandparents were right. If you want something, there is nothing wrong with a little sacrifice and saving. If it is important, you will do just that, save for it. Our easy credit society has made us lose our understanding of the value of money. It has to stop now. Nothing will stop you from reaching your financial goals more than debt. I am sorry if I am going sound like a wet blanket or even worse, un-American, by saying this, but I HATE DEBT! I hate it! I hate it! I hate it! Debt is crippling. It is dead weight that will slow you down from achieving your dreams.

There are those—mostly bankers, credit card companies, and merchants—who will argue, "Debt is a tool. It is a way that you can get what you need now, in low monthly payments. It helps the economy because more money is moving around." Wrong! Debt is not a tool! Debt is a blight on the American economy and more specific to you, it will ruin your financial plan. If you need $1 million to retire (which you might), how are you going to get there if you owe over $20,000 between your car payments and credit cards? I'll show you how to get the $1 million to retire on, but you can't start saving until your debt is gone.

If you have a considerable amount of debt, not including your house, then you need help right now. When I say a considerable amount of debt, I mean any debt at all. I am of the mind that no personal debt is good. If you have a car payment, credit card payments, owe a medical firm, or are renting to own furniture, it is too much debt.   We have come to believe as Americans that debt is a way of life. When I say deal with your debt, I mean eliminate it and never take it on again. Nothing good can come from debt. As Dave Ramsey, personal finance guru, states, "I am not against spending money. I am against spending money you don't have." Here here!

Death to Credit Cards

It is amazing how pervasive credit cards are. Most of my mail is delivered to a P.O. Box I only check about once a week. Each week, with outfail, I get 3 to 5 applications for new cards. I'm sure you get the same. Most people think: *I must be able to afford the credit, if they are willing to give me the card.* Wrong! It is important to understand how credit card companies make their money.

First, they make money on every transaction they process. The credit card company gets between one half and three percent of each transaction. The merchant selling the products or services you buy, pays this fee. For example, if a store is paying a two percent fee on purchases and you buy $100 of product the credit card company pays the store $98. The second way the credit card company makes money is off the interest they charge the card holder. If you pay your full bill each month, then you accrue no charges. If you don't, you are then charged interest on the balance you are carrying. This can be as high as 25 percent or more! So do you really think a credit card company wants you to pay off your debt to them? They are not offering you credit you can afford. They benefit by offering you more than you can afford, so they can make money on your interest payments.

You should not use credit cards, *for anything*. If you don't believe me then believe this: a British banking executive was asked, during an investigation by the British government into credit card fees, if he used credit cards. He said he didn't. When pressed as to why, he told the panel that the interest rates were way too high. If the person whose salary, which I will assume is much more than yours or mine—and is paid by these fees—thinks they are too much, we might take a cue from that.

Besides making it very easy to accrue debt at a very high interest rate, credit cards have a second problem, they mask how much you are spending. I used to use credit cards all the time. Many times when I signed the receipt I didn't even look to see how much I was paying. This can be folly in two ways. First, it's very easy to sign a slip that is more than what you should be paying. Second, you have no real sense of what you are spending day to day because you don't feel the budget pinch until its too late.

Pay Cash All the Time

You should pay cash for everything with the possible exception of buying a home. There are a number of benefits to paying cash. First, when you pay cash, you know if you can afford the purchase because you have the cash in hand. If you don't have the cash, then you can't afford it. Second, you are much more likely to get a deal with cash. If you working with a salesperson that has a quota to meet and you have cash in hand, he will be more likely to make a deal. When you have cash in hand, you are in the power seat of the negotiation (see section on bargaining to see how). Finally, it is much easier to understand how much something is really worth to you when you are paying cash for it. The shirt you want costs $80. It is much harder to give the clerk four twenties, than it is to hand over a piece of plastic. You know how hard you work to get the cash. As you hold the cash in your hand, you will see it value. It's amazing. When you do this, you're much less likely to spend money.

If you're not comfortable carrying lots of cash around, use a debit card. Debit cards look just like credit cards. You can do just about everything with a debit card that you can with a credit card. It works the same as cash. With a debit card you can't send the money you don't have. The only drawback to debit cards, is you don't see as accurately how you are spending your money.

Step 2: Calculating Debt

The second step to stopping the leaks is also the first step to creating your budget. In this step, you will calculate how much debt you have. In order to have a clear plan how to kill this debt, you must know the monster you are fighting. Also, you need to understand where you stand right now, before you can start planning how you will spend your money. On a clean sheet of paper in your notebook, write down every debt you have, how much you owe, what the monthly payments are, and what the interest rate is. Make sure you include every debt you have.

- car payments
- student loans
- credit cards
- any financed purchase (tires, furniture, roof)
- money owed to the doctor or dentist
- money owed to family members and friends

The next step is to list the debts in order of highest interest rate to the lowest rate. Obviously, the debt that is costing you the most, is worst. When you finish this list, I have a feeling you might be a little overwhelmed. You might be feeling stress. This is all the more reason to eliminate your debt. When you are in debt, in some way, your life is not your own. Someone else holds you. Getting rid of debt will give you freedom. If freeing yourself from the stress is not enough of an incentive to take radical measures to get rid of your debt, consider the numbers: Let's pretend that right now you are making $700 in debt payment a month in credit cards and car payments. If you get rid of your debt, it is the same thing as getting a $8400 raise. If you weren't paying debt, you would have $700 a month to spend on other things. Even better, that's

If you are making $700 in debt payments a month and you eliminate your debt, it is the same as getting a $8400 raise.

money that you could be saving for a down payment on your house, pay for college tuition, or to save for retirement. You will see how powerful $700 a month can be towards meeting your goals.

CALCULATING DEBT
- Make a list of every debt that you have (except your house).
- For each debt, list the amount you owe, the interest rate, and the minimum monthly payment.
- Re-order the list from highest interest rate to lowest interest rate.

Step 3: Determining Where Your Money Is Going

Before you can create a budget, you need an accurate understanding of where your money is going now. This is the next step toward creating an effective budget—a budget based on where you actually spend your money. First, by looking at your current spending habits, you'll identify all of the spending that cannot be changed (at least in the short term). For example, if you are a homeowner, there is a minimum you have to pay each month towards a mortgage. Second, by looking at your current spending you'll identify *wasteful spending*. Wasteful spending is defined as any spending that is hurting your ability to creating a life you can live with passion. Finally, you will change your spending habits. This becomes much easier when you recognize the drag wasteful spending is putting on your financial planning.

In order to get a sense of where your money is going, you'll need to do a little research. The more data you have, the more accurate your conclusions will be. For example, knowing your average monthly spending over the last six months, will be much more helpful than knowing how you spent your money in just one month, say December. Six months of data should give you enough information to create your first month's budget.

The first step is to gather all of the information. You'll need bank statements, canceled checks, and credit card statements from the last six months. From this information, you should be able to track where most of your money has gone. These records should be in one place. If they aren't, create a system to use from this moment forward. The system doesn't have to be complicated. It can be nothing more than a few file folders. I recommend folders for bank statements, investment, credit card bills, pay stubs, and past tax forms. You never know when you will need them (like if, God forbid, the IRS comes knocking on your door).

You don't need to keep four years of phone bills, the canceled checks will be enough.

If you pay your bills and then throw them away, you only have a vague idea of how much money is in your checking account at any one time. If you balance your check book by looking at your bank statement each month to see if you have any money left, don't panic! This process will just take you a little longer. This section will help you create the good habits you need to manage your money. In the short term, gather up as much information as you can. If that is only this month's worth of bills and cancelled checks, it's a start. This is only to create a baseline. As you move forward, you'll gather the information you'll need for a more accurate picture of your spending.

If you *do* have the data for six months, *use the data for six months*! Yes, it will be more work, but the more data you use as your baseline, the easier it will be to create an accurate budget. This will make living with your budget much easier.

The second step is to figure out where every cent you have spent has gone in the last six months. To do this, you are will categorize every expenditure you have made. I would start by collecting the information in your notebook. Use a separate page for each category. These categories should be big and broad such as home, entertainment, car, tuition, and insurance. Go through each canceled check, ATM withdrawal, and credit card statement. Take every single expense and add it to one of the categories. Write down the expense, the date of the transaction, and how much it was for.

The third step, after you written down all of the expenses by category, is to create sub-categories. For example, in the home category you would have food, gas, water, phone, and electric sub-categories. Total up the sub-categories and divide by six (or the number of months you have data for). This will give you an average of how much you spend each month in each sub-category.

The next step is to move all of the data to a master budget sheet (see sample on next page). Create the Master Budget sheet in your notebook. You will notice on the Master Budget Sheet that there are four columns. The information you have just gathered will be used to fill the first two columns. The first column is for the list of all your sub-categories. In the second column, write the average amount for the sub-category.

For the fifth step, you need to add all of your debts to the Master Budget Sheet. This is the list you created in the last step. For all of the debts, write the minimum payment in the second column.

Finally, there is one more piece of information to add to your Master Budget Sheet before you can create your new budget. That information is your current

NOTE: THIS IS ONLY A SAMPLE MASTER BUDGE SHEET TO GIVE AN IDEA OF WHAT IT SHOULD LOOK LIKE. THIS IS NOT A COMPREHENSIVE LIST OF CATEGORIES

MASTER BUDGET SHEET

PAYMENTS
HOME
    HOME PAYMENT
    GAS
    ELECTRIC
    PHONE
    CABLE
    WATER
    FOOD
    CELL PHONE

AUTO
    CAR PAYMENT
    GAS
    MAINTENANCE
    OIL CHANGE
    INSURANCE

PERSONAL
    LIFE INSURANCE
    HEALTH INSURANCE
    SAVINGS
    TITHING

OTHER DEBT
    CREDIT CARD 1
    CREDIT CARD 2
    MEDICAL BILL
    FAMILY MEMBER

TOTAL

INCOME
    INCOME 1
    INCOME 2
    OTHER INCOME

TOTAL

income. In the income section at the bottom, add every type of regular income your household receives. It is important that you list your post-tax pay (also know as "take home pay"). You want to build your budget off of the money you have to spend.

This process could take an hour or two to complete. It works best to set a good chunk of time aside to do this work in one sitting. Before you begin, make sure you have all information you need. Yes, wasting a couple of hours of a Saturday afternoon looking at old bills is not my first choice, but remember why we are doing this. Your dreams are worth the effort.

CALCULATING EXPENDITURES
- Gather six months of spending data.
- Categorize every expenditure
- Divide into subcategories
- Total and average each subcategory.
- Transfer data to Master Budget Sheet.
- List all debts on the Master Budget Sheet
- List take home pay on the Master Budget Sheet

Step 4: Creating a Budget You Can Live With

Before you construct your budget, look very closely at your debt and your spending habits. For most of us it is difficult to add more income to our lives (though in some cases we will see this is necessary). The two easiest ways to balance your budget are eliminating debt and eliminating wasteful spending. Your budget will help you do these things which will, in turn, make it easier to meet your other financial goals. Later we will talk about how to adjust your budget once you are debt free for investing, retirement, buying a home, and sending your kids to college.

How Much Is That $4 cup of Coffee Worth

If you did the last two steps well, then you should be able to see there are a number of simple things you can do to start saving money now. The easiest place to start is with the dead weight (and I don't mean those extra 15 lbs you might be carrying around your mid-section). I am talking about all spending that is not adding value to your life. They may bring a little short term happiness, but no real value.*

*I am not saying that little things to make us smile are bad things to have in our life, it is just important to understand what those things cost.

For an example, let's talk about everyone's favorite cup of coffee from Fourbucks. Don't get me wrong, I enjoy a "a medium triple white mocha decaf soy extra hot with whip" as much as the next person, but do you really *need* it and the caffeine addiction you have now acquired. Let's say on your way to work 5 days a week you buy a $4 cup of coffee. Take that and multiply it 52 weeks. Every year you are spending—drum roll please—$1050 a year on coffee. Is that cup of coffee you had this morning worth $1050? If you said yes, then you might want to look into counseling.

There may come a time in your life where it will be the land of milk and honey, or coffee and biscotti if you will, but if you are serious about getting your financial life in order, this is probably not that time. After taking all the time to figure out where your money is currently going (the last step), it gives you the opportunity to ask the questions about your spending, such as, *Would I be willing to give up cable TV in my home for $480 this year?* For me, the answer was yes. It is very important in this step, as you craft your budget, to understand what each of these expenditures is worth to you. These questions become even more important as you look to eliminate debt.

Eliminating Your Debt

The question comes, *How much of my budget should be set aside to kill debt?* I would say every cent possible. The sooner you get rid of your debt, the better off you will be. Are you getting the feeling I hate debt? Good! You should too. Debt prevents you from crafting a life you can live with passion. It prevents you from travel, buying a home, or a car. Debt adds stress in your life that you don't need. The sooner you can get rid of it, the richer your life can become. When you do your budgeting, you should cut everything you don't need from your life until your debt is gone. Give up beer. Give up chocolate. Give up the family vacation. Every dollar you don't spend, is a dollar closer to being out of debt. Get rid of the cable. Not only will you save some money; you might rediscover the joy of conversation. Don't get me wrong, I am not saying you need to cut the fun out of your life. I am just saying you need to be a little more creative. You can have as much fun at the park with your family as you can a Chuck E. Cheese's. It's a matter of developing new habits—less expensive habits that keep a life you can live with passion in mind.

The plan of attack you'll use to eliminating your debt fast, is simple. You will pay the minimum payment on every single piece of debt except the one that is at the highest rate. If you copied your list of debts from the sheet you did your debt calculation on to the Master Budget Sheet, it will be the debt at the top of your debt list. For that debt you will pay everything you have left over from your budget. You are to do this every month. Once the first debt is paid off, you will move to the second debt on your list, which should be the debt with the second highest interest rate. Again, you will pay the minimum payment for all your debts except for this one. Every cent that is left over in your budget will go to this debt until it is gone. You will continue this process until you are debt free.

SIDE NOTE: As we talked about in the first half of the book, even when we make the choice to make a change oftentimes we need a little extra incentive to make the change. Try this. Place this list of all your debt in some visible place. Put it on the fridge or the wall near your computer. Just like Chris looking at the picture of his daughter, I want you to look at this all the time, so you know why you are living by a tighter budget. The system I have just explained has you paying off the debt on the top of the list first. Once the first debt is fully paid off, I would recommend, with a thick red marker, draw a line through the piece of debt you just killed. Not only having the list up will remind you why you are making the choices you are making, but it will also give you incentive by showing you your progress. After you cross a debt off. I would also recommend you do the "I-just-killed-the-debt-happy-dance," but that is up to you.

You must understand debt is your enemy. You must be willing to go to any means necessary to get rid of it. Like I said, get rid of the cable, stop buying expensive gourmet coffee, and don't go on vacation until your debt is gone. Take the radical step of getting a second job. If you are thinking to yourself, "I can't do this. This is too hard." If you think, "This is not fair that I have to sacrifice." Tough Cookies! Even if you aren't responsible for your current situation, it is still your situation. It is entirely possible that you are in a situation where you are making less money than you need, just to make the minimum payments. If this is the case, I am not going to lie, you are in real trouble. You work is cut out for you. If this is the case, you need to find more income. One of my favorite radio moments of all time, happened on a personal finance call-in show. I wish I could remember who the host was, because how he handled the situation was just brilliant. A woman called in and said something like (I am just making up the number so you get the point), "Right now I have about $27,000 in debt and the creditors are calling all the time." The host asked how much she made a month. "I make about $400 a week after taxes working part time." The host suggested that she find a second job. "I can't do that." The host tried to explain that her problem wasn't going to go away unless she found another job. "I just can't do that. It would be too hard to find another job and really inconvenient." This is when the moment of radio brilliance happened. The host simply said, "I am sorry. I can't help you. Next caller."

The only one who can do anything about your situation is you. If you are not capable of working hard for the next two years (yes, I said two years) to kill your debt, then I don't know what to tell you. Nothing after this point in the book will help you unless you take your debt problem seriously. You can't live a life with passion, unless you take control of your life. You would never put nice furniture in a house that has gaping holes in the ceiling, and you can't have a life you can live with passion until your plug the holes that are debt.

Creating Your New Budget

Now that we have spent a little time talking about the two lenses you should use as you start to create your budget—eliminate wasteful spending and eliminating debt—it is now time to start building your first month's budget. The reason that I use the term "first month budget" is because the budget you create now is only the start. The budget you are about to create will be based off of averages of your spending, and what you think you can cut from your budget. After a month, you might discover that you can cut even deeper in some areas, while others you have cut too deep. This will require you to reconfigure your budget.

Use the third column to create the budget you will live on for the next month. The way the budget will work is simple. You will not spend more money than you have. It would be a good idea to keep a calculator handy as you do this part. Basically, what you will do is decide how much you will spend on each subcategory for the next month, insuring you total expenses don't exceed your income.

The first step is to add all the information to the third column that is fixed. This information includes your income, the minimum payment amount on all your debts except the first one, and any expense that is fixed from month to month, such as the cable bill, life insurance.

It is time to figure out what you will spend on everything else. Remember your first goal is to get rid of debt. The less money you spend on daily expenses the more you will be able to use to pay down your debt. In the third column, write down how much you will spend on each item. For each of your monthly expenses, take a look at the average you have spent over the last six months. The question you need to ask yourself is, *"Is having x in my life worth this much money?"* This is the moment where you will be tested to see how serious you are about getting out of debt. Is it going to be hard to makes these cuts? Yes, it is. When our friends have the latest fashion, do we want to have them as well? Yes. When our friends go out to eat, do we what to join them? Yes. It will be hard to make the choices that are right for you. But if you want to have a life you can live with passion, then you will have to make the choices that make the most sense for you. I will warn you, choosing what to cut is the easy part. *Yes*, I mean that. The hard part will be sticking to the budget that you create.

After you have made decision on how much you will spend on each subcategory, you should only have one blank left on your form. That blank should be after the first debt. This is the debt you will pay off first. You will commit every extra cent you have from your income to this debt, to kill it as fast as you can. To calculate what to write on this line, add up all your expenses and subtract that value from your total income.

At this point one of two things has happened. First, and less likely, you have created a completely unrealistic budget for yourself. You have the passion of killing debt in your soul, and you have decided that you don't need to eat lunch this month, giving you more money to kill debt. If this is the case, I love your passion, but you do need to eat. Or second, and more likely, you are not very impressed with the amount of money committed to debt you will kill. The last step of creating the budget is go back and start tweaking the numbers. It is important that you do this in a realistic manner. It is important to cut, but if it is not realistic then you have nothing more than a pretty budget that is impossible to fulfill (something like the federal government would create). Go back and look at each subcategory and see if you can trim a little more. Maybe your first version of the budget has you going out to eat twice a month as a family. Eliminate one of those outings and you will have $50 (or more) to contribute to the elevation of your debt. The goal is to end up with a budget that you can live with, that has the largest amount possible going to eliminating your debt.

WRITING YOUR BUDGET

- In column three, write all of the fixed expenses for the month
- Considering the six month averages, write how much you will send for each subcategory.
- Add all your expenditures and subtract this value from your total income. This amount is the budget value for your first debt.
- Revisit each expense to see if you can realistically make more cuts.
- Recalculate the amount you will pay to your first debt.

Step 5: Living with your budget

This is where it gets hard, and I mean really hard. This is where you will have to start to live your budget. When we are working in some abstract sense of creating a budget on paper, it is easy. I can go without this and that, but three days later that motivation is gone and you are spending money in a way that is not congruent with what you want for your life. No matter how hard this seems, you can do this! You have everything you need as part of your character to do this, especially if you remember why you are making the choice you are making. I know I keep harping on this point, but it's important. It is why the book you are holding in your hands is different from the other financial books you could buy. You need to keep the vision of a life you can live with passion, in the front of your mind.

When I was creating a budget for myself, one of the decisions I made was that I was no longer going to buy candy. That didn't mean I gave up candy all together. I would let other people give me candy, but I wasn't going to spend my own money on it. That is a great idea, but at three in the afternoon when you are standing in the candy aisle and hundreds of candy bars in their bright wrappers are looking up at you, it's hard. The way I was able to stop myself (most of the time) was to tell myself over and over again, "You don't need this candy bar. The money in your pocket is earmarked for a trip to Iceland. Something you really want." I know that seventy-nine cents is not going to make the difference between me going to Iceland and not. If I am able to make the right choice over and over again, it will make a difference in the long run. You will have to keep reminding yourself constantly why you are making the sacrifices you are making. As you live with you budget, just remember how these decisions effect your ability to live the life you really want.

There are a few things to keep in mind when it comes to your budget. First, from this day forward you will run a zero sum budget or better. This means that you will never spend more than you make ever again. If one of your budget lines grows, one will have to shrink. For example, you decide that you need a new pair of shoes because your right shoe has a giant hole. The problem is that you have spent all the money you have budgeted for clothing for the month. You have two choices. Get out the duct tape to hold the shoes together or you need to cut how much you spend on the shoes from something else. It is very simple. From this day forward, you are going keep moving forward because you can and more importantly, you deserve to.

Second, just because you have created this budget, doesn't mean that you are magically going to have will power. It is easy to fall back into bad habits. You can create a situation where the choices you face are easier. Two of my best friends have created a plan to keep from going out to dinner. The church service they attend is at 5:15 on Sunday night. Afterwards, lots of folks head out to dinner. In order to stop themselves from being tempted to join their friends, before going to the church they put together dinner in the crock-pot and start it. When their friends ask them to go out they say, "We would love to, but we already have dinner going in the crock-pot at home." Is hanging out with friends a bad thing? No. Is eating good food a sin? No. Before my friends were going out to dinner after church twice a month. By cooking dinner in the crock-pot they save $80 a month or close to $1000 a year.

Third, you might fail. This should be really hard if you are only paying cash for everything, because it is impossible to spend cash you don't have. You should strive with every means possible not to fail. I know you can do it without failing, but if you do stumble, don't kill yourself over it. Take a step back. Look at the situation. See why you failed. Learn from the experience. Re-adjust your budget. Don't make the same mistake again. Move on. Like I said before, guilt is debilitating and regret is instructive.

Fourth, the way you can tell if you are living your budget is by utilizing the fourth column of the Master Budget. At the end of the month, calculate how much you have sent in each of the subcategories. More often than not, the first budget is not exactly how the month will work out. After you have gathered all the data from the first month of living your budget, take a hard look at how you spent your money. From this information, it is now time to create the next month's budget. On a clean Master Budget Sheet, based off the new information of living your budget for one month, write what you will spend in each subcategory. Do this every month for the rest of your life. Really, for the rest of your life. As time passes it will be easier and easier. Debt will go away. The house will get paid off. You might receive a raise. Just because you get your money situation under control, doesn't mean you can be cavalier about your spending. You should always choose exactly where you want all your money to go. If you are going to part with your money thoughtlessly, send it to me.

Fifth, as time passes, you will pay off your first debt. At this point, the next step is easy. All of the money that has been freed up by killing the first debt is now applied to the second debt. Your debt-killing process will speed up and gain momentum as you go! Close your eyes for a moment. Think of the day when you make your last debt payment. You have spent months and months paying hundreds of dollars to creditors. All of a sudden, you are free. Not only are you free, you now have that money to spend on other things.

Finally, a note if you are married. If you are married, not only should you create a budget together, but you should make sure each month you are meeting about the budget together. At least once a month, you and your spouse should have a budget meeting, where the two of you pay all the bills together. I would also recommend that one person can't break the budget (reallocate funds from one area to another) without the consent of the other. Money can be a very stressful topic, especially when you don't feel in control of your future. I can't stress enough that you need to be on the same page when it comes to money. One way many couples choose to create a little flexibility in the budget is to set aside a small amount for each person to do whatever they want with. It can be as small as forty or fifty dollars a month. By being on the same page, you will reach your goals sooner and you will fight less.

LIVING WITH YOUR BUDGET

- Run a zero sum budget or better. From this day forward, you will not spend more than you have—ever.
- Find ways which make it easier for you to live by your budget
- When you fail to understand the mistakes you have made, learn from them, and try again.
- Every month, track your spending to make sure you are living within your budget
- Readjust your budget, as necessary, over time.
- After you kill your first debt, go after the second and then the third until you are debt free
- If you are married, hold a monthly budget meeting in which you pay all of this month's bills and plan for next month's budget.

LONG TERM EMERGENCY FUND

If you follow through on your budgeting, you will, in a systematic fashion, eliminate debt from your life. In our analogy, you have taken care of the leaks. Once you eliminate your debt, you will now have more money to spend. In keeping with our analogy, before we can run out and furnish the house, AKA "buying stuff" with this extra money, we need to make sure we take care of the foundation for the future. The first thing you need to do with your extra money is to take care of your long-term emergency fund.

Long Term Emergency Fund

Once you eliminated your debt, it is time to build your long term emergency fund. Your short term emergency fund was built to take care of small emergencies such as car repair or the fixing the dishwasher. Now is the time to prepare for major emergencies, such as you or your spouse losing a job. Most financial planners and consultants will recommend your long term emergency fund be equal to three to six months of your household expenses. It is important to note that I said three to six months of *household expenses*. I did not say three to six months of income. If you loose your job, you will still need to make payments on your house. You still need food, heat, and electricity. At the same time, you will put your retirement savings on hold. Retirement is still a concern, but it is the least of your concerns in a moment of real emergency. Therefore, when you determine the number of month's worth of savings, you will base the actual amount of savings on your household expenses.

How much you decide to have in your fund will depend on you. There are a number of factors which will play into how large of a long term fund you will need. Because each life is different, there are no hard and fast rules. If you are a single income home (single or married) your fund should be closer to six months because of the dependence you have on the one income. Also, if you are self-employed or working on commission, you should also have a larger fund because you are more likely to have inconsistent income. If you are in a job with stability, such as a tenured teacher or government worker, you are much less likely to face trouble and are able to have a smaller fund.

The final, and most important, factor in determining the size of the long term fund you need, is your level of ability to deal with risk. Your emergency fund is just like the safety blanket you had as a child. I know I always felt safer when I had my blanket. Just knowing it was there kept the monsters under the bed at bay. You long term fund works in the same way. It has two goals. First, and primary, is to take care of emergencies. But second, and equally important, it purchases your piece of mind. If you are really worried about catastrophe have more in your fund. Don't feel embarrassed if you have a low level of risk tolerance. Do what you need to do to feel secure. For example, you are going to be more comfortable with a smaller fund if you are only taking care of yourself. Everything changes when you have kids. You are no longer just worrying about yourself, but your whole family. At this point, you are going feel much less likely to want to take the risk, so you create a larger fund.

You don't need to maintain short term and long term funds. Once you have taken care of your debt, your short term fund becomes the long term fund. Like the short term emergency fund, all the same rules apply to this money. Take the money you were using to pay off your debt, and add it each month to your emergency fund account. Do this until you have saved enough money to meet your fund needs. Also, like the short term fund you built, it should only be used in *real* emergencies. If you use money from the fund, replenish it as soon as you can. By this, I mean putting your other savings (retirement and college) on hold until the fund in rebuilt. Finally, only use the money in this fund after a great amount of consideration (and agreement, if you are married).

BUILDING A LONG TERM EMERGENCY FUND
- Determine the size of the fund you would like to create.
- Add all the extra money from your budget to the emergency fund.
- Only use the money in time of emergency.
- If you do use money from the emergency fund, put all other saving on hold until the fund is rebuilt.

Update Your Résumé

You should update your resume about once a year. This is an important part of emergency planning. More than likely, you are a bit of realist and understand we live in uncertain times. Realistically, all times are uncertain. Ours just feel more uncertain because we are facing the uncertainty. Even the greatest, most secure companies in the world can disappear quickly. Losing your job is not something to dwell on, but it is a real possibility. If job lose comes suddenly, it is going add a lot of stress to your life. If you have taken care of your emergency fund, it will be less stressful, but it will still be stressful.

I think there are three main advantages to having an up-to-date résumé. First, like many things in life, it is easier to maintain something than it is to create it. Creating a résumé from scratch can be time consuming. Once it is written, it can take less than an hour a year to maintain. Second, if you do lose your job, it is one less thing to worry about. One thing we as humans are very good at, is denial. I know in my life I have become a master at hiding from the problems I have. When we create artificial barriers to a solution, we don't have to face the problem. In the case of job loss, there is a lot of emotional baggage. You might feel like you are a failure because you lost your job regardless of the situation. You will think to yourself, "If I was only better at my job I wouldn't have lost it." When you have to look for a new job, you have to face square on the fact that you lost your old job. So we don't have to feel that pain again and again, we create an obstacle preventing us from looking for a job. "I can't look for a job yet because I don't have a résumé. As soon as I update it, I will start looking." I am not saying the moment you lose a job, you need to start looking for the next one. If you have done a good job with your emergency fund, it will afford some time for perspective, but this can't last forever. You can't just sit at home watching soaps all day. That is *not* looking for perspective. You will need to find work. Being unemployed is stressful enough without having to worry about putting together a résumé. By having your résumé current, you are one step closer (and you have removed one more hurdle before you start looking for a job). Finally, you might be in a situation where you want to change jobs. By having a résumé, it is very easy to do a little shopping in the job market. For example, your dream job comes up out of the blue, instead of having to scramble, you are set.

There are loads of books on how to write a résumé. Almost all of them are adequate. It may take a few weeks to get a good résumé crafted, but in the long run it is really worth it. If you live near your college alma mater, many times you can get free résumé help from their career center, regardless how long ago you graduated. A curent résumé will strengthen your safety net.

RETIREMENT

The analogy continues...So far you have gotten out of the rain (short term emergency fund), plugged the leaks (eliminated debt and wasteful spending) and worked on the foundation (long term emergency fund). It is time to start thinking about the future of the house. You can start to do the major part of your savings and plan for retirement.

Do You Want to Retire?

The title of this book really should have been HOW TO SAVE THE WORLD AND RETIRE (IF YOU WANT TO). If you think about it, retirement is really a modern concept. As a practical part of life, the idea is really less than a hundred years old. Up until very recently you basically worked until you couldn't any more, then a few years later you were dead. At the time retirement at 65 started becoming part of American life, most folks didn't live until 65. For those few who did live that long, they were cared for by their families or got by on social security for their last few years.

Today, that is not the case. The average life expectancy in the US was just moved to 77.4 years. People commonly live into their eighties or much older. Retirement is no longer the last few years of your life, but can be as many as 20 years or more. Before we start talking about what you need to do to make sure that you are financially stable enough to retire, it is important to understand what you want your "retirement years" to look like. Do you really want to clock into work one last time, clean out your desk, take your gold watch, and head home to play cards every day? I don't know if I could handle that lifestyle. I have been on vacations where the first three days sitting in a beach chair doing nothing was just what I needed, but by day seven I was ready to get back to my life, and of all things, get back to work.

Often the notion is when we retire, we would like to travel the world or write a book. Why do those things have to wait until you retire? It might be hard to leave your daily life right now for 18 months to see the whole country in a Holiday Rambler, but you could see Europe next year. Why defer the fun stuff? You have no idea how your health is going to be in the future. Or you might be in a situation where, as your parents age, you might choose to be their caregiver, which would prevent you from following those dreams. Don't defer. Do it now. I have read story after story about retirees who had a really hard time with retirement. Many of them feel like they had lost their identity when they left their work. They become depressed without purpose. I am not contending that retirement is bad or that you should plan to work for the rest of your life, unless you would like to. My hope is that my retirement years are the opportunity to only do the work that I want to do. You should build a financial plan that allows you do what you like, with little concern for money. I can't imagine that I am ever going to stop doing work that I love. I have always loved the work I have done, and I enjoy being around people a lot. But, if I take care of my finances properly I will be able to do work I love, such as working for a non-profit, and take no payment at all. Simply do the work out of a sense of love.

How Much Will You Need to Retire?

After careful consideration of what you would like your retirement to look like the next logical question is, *"How much money will I need to retire?"* Let's do some calculations. To keep it simple, we will make four assumptions for our example and do the calculations in terms of today's dollar. This means we are not going to take into account inflation or cost of living increase. Remember, this is just a rough estimate. First, you want to maintain the same quality of living you have right now. Second, currently you make $30,000 a year. Third, your housing cost is going to be the same. Hopefully by the time you retire, your home will be paid off. Finally, let's assume that you will not have any work related income. Since you will not be working, you will need to have enough money saved that the return on the investment replaces your income. In this case, that mean the return on your investment needs to be $30,000 a year. If you were able to invest your retirement savings (in a diversified manner) at 6% you will need to have a cool $500,000 saved at retirement age. $500,000 returning 6% a year will produce $30,000 in dividend. That may seem daunting because it is, but only a little. If nothing else, it means you need to start now.

RETIREMENT CALCULATOR
- Current income ÷ 0.06 = Amount you need to retire

Note: *Remember this is a very rough estimate to give you an idea of the saving you will need.*

Social Security

You might think, "Well, I really don't need that much, because I will also have my Social Security benefits." Brace yourself. Social security will not be around when you retire. Okay, that is not entirely true. It would be political suicide for any group of politicians to let social security die, but by the time it comes for you and I to get any benefits, there will be so little money left that it will help you very little in your retirement planning. It is best to assume that it won't be there. You don't believe me? Read on.

The reason that Social Security won't be around is because how it is constructed. Basically, what happens is while you are working age, you pay into the fund. The money in the fund is used to pay the benefits for those who have paid into the fund in the past and are now retired. When it comes time for you to retire your benefits are paid out of the money the current work force is paying. All this time the money in the fund is being invested at a low rate to generate some income. There are a number of flaws with this system. First, in order to entice you to put money into any fund, there needs to be the promise that more money is going to be paid out in the end. Since the money in the fund returns a low rate, in order to be able to generate more money for benefits the government raises the amount of money that the current work force is putting into the fund. In order to keep raising the benefits for future generations, the amount of contribution of current workers put into the fund will have to keep going up. The second problem is the fact that people are having less and less children. Once everyone's favorite, the baby boomers, reach retirement age there will be more people retired than in the work force. This means there will come a day in which every member of the work forces contributing to Social Security will have to support more than one retiree. One of two things will have to happen. Either fund contribution will have to keep rising, benefit pay out will decrease, the age benefits will be paid out will raise, or all three. At the printing of this book, Congress was considering raising the retirement age to 73 and reduce the benefits to anyone who was considered affluent. The debate has the current definition of being *affluent* as anyone who makes more than $50,000 a year.

If you read these facts carefully you will understand a simple point: Social Security is a giant pyramid scheme. I am not joking about this. You get benefits once there are people younger than you working. At a certain point, there are not enough people paying into the fund for the people at the top of the pyramid to keep receiving benefits. If I were to open a private plan that was set up in the same fashion, I would be arrested. Pyramid schemes are illegal because they cannot succeed.

A conversation about what needs to happen to solve the Social Security problem is much too large of a discussion to have here. The one point that is important is when you are making your retirement planning; assume Social Security will not be there. If there is any money at all, consider it a pleasant surprise and nothing more.

The Power of Compound Interest

I have the feeling you are freaking out. So far I have told you to get rid of every piece of debt you have, you will need a lot more than you thought to retire, and the safety net of Social Security will not be there. If that was the total story, I would be freaking out now as well. Relax. It is not the total story because you have, at your disposal, the greatest power in the universe. Well, at least in the financial universe. You have the power of compound interest. You need to put your math hat on for a few minutes to understand this, but don't worry. I will keep it simple, because compound interest is simple.

I assume you understand what interest is. If not, no big deal. I will go slowly. As a refresher, let's look at loans and savings accounts as an example of how interest rates (or rates of return) work, but remember the math is the same on all types of investments. Interest is nothing more than a fee a borrower pays to use someone else's money. Many times this payment is a percentage of the total amount. When you get a mortgage, you borrow money from the bank and pay them a fee, the interest, for the use of their money. When you open a savings account, your money does not sit in some box in the back with your name on it. In reality the bank is borrowing money from you so it can give loans and make investments. They pay you a fee, the interest, to use your money. Compound interest is nothing more than receiving interest on the principle, the original amount of money, and receiving interest on the previous interest payments.

For example, let assume you have $100 in a savings account that is getting an interest payment of 7.2% a year. The first year you would receive an interest payment of $7.20. Instead of taking that money out to buy a movie ticket, you decide to leave the interest in the bank. The next year you would receive an interest payment on the $107.20 (your $100 plus the $7.20 interest payment) which is $7.72. You might be thinking, "Wow! That is powerful; I just made an extra fifty-two cents. I feel like the most powerful force in the universe. Thanks Gene for unleashing this power in my life." Patience, we are just getting started.

The math will show us, at 7.2% in ten years your investment will double. So after 10 years, with compound interest, you will have about $200. In ten more years, you will double that amount again to $400. It is important to note the second time we doubled the amount, we didn't double just the principle (your original $100), but the whole amount. So after twenty years, we are at $400. Yes, I know you could have made more than $300 collecting cans for 20 years, but stay with me. After thirty years, we are at $800, after forty years we are at $1600, and after fifty years we are at $3200. $3200 will not be enough to retire on, but the example shows, over time, how compound interest starts to grow money in a powerful way. Still unconvinced? Let's look at a real world example.

Let's say that you are 40 years old and you have decided to invest $100 a month for your retirement. The market over the long term pays an average of 10%. Pay attention, here are two important points! First, it is important to understand that in order to take advantage of the market's growth, you must be invested over the long haul. The market goes up and down, but over time has gone up. If you are in for the long haul and not trying to time the ups and downs, you should be safe. More details will be given in the next few sections. Second, past performance does not guarantee future results. To keep the math simple, we will assume you are only going to make one payment a year of $1200 (equal to $100 a month). At 10% money will double every 7.2 years. Also, in this example you are not only getting gains from the interest, but also you are adding to the principle each year. After ten years you will have invested $12,000 ($100 a month X 12 months X 10 years = $12,000) and will have value of $25,661.14, a little more than double your investment. After twenty years, you will have invested $24,000 and will have a value of $85,683.30, more than triple your investment. This is where it get really interesting. At sixty five, five years later, you will have invested $30,000 but your investment will now be worth $145,319.90. That is more than four times your investment. This example was done, starting a little late and only saving $100 a month.

One more example for the non-believers out there. The force behind compound interest is time. The more time passes, the more times your money will double itself. Here is an example my father showed me of how seven years can make a huge difference. For this example, we are going take a set of twin brothers, Gregory and Smegory. At age 18, Gregory starts saving $1200 a year and is earning 10%. He makes these payments for seven years, then stops. Even though he is not making payments he keeps his money invested earning 10%. Smegory on the other had doesn't start investing until 25, the day Gregory stops. Smegory makes the exact same investment and makes payments until he is sixty five. At sixty five Gregory has invested $8400 and Smegory has invested $49,200. The question is, *Who is worth more?* Smegory, of course. Did you think it was some sort of trick question? With that being said, the difference between the two is very little. With the scenarios I have just painted, Smegory is worth $643,964.39 and Gregory, investing more than $40,000 less, is worth $623,463.10. Gregory invested much less than his brother, but he had the extra time. That is the power of compound interest. If Gregory would have invest $1200 from eighteen and not stopped at twenty five, but kept invested until he was sixty-five, his investment would be worth $1,267,427.49. Starting seven year earlier would be the difference of over $600,000. The message, start now! Let's take a look at how you can take advantage of compound interest.

Pay Yourself First

The concern most people have about investing is, "Where is the money going to come from?" Having money to invest for retirement is easy if you have followed the steps up to this point. By eliminating debt you will free up money, which had been going to finance your debt. When you pay cash and stick to your budget, you insure that you are not adding any new debt. After you have built your emergency fund, you will use this money to invest for retirement. By doing all these steps saving for retirement is easy, all you have to do is pay yourself first.

Multiple studies and surveys have shown time and again that people spend what they have, regardless how much they make. Former NBA start Patrick Ewing once said about his need for a raise in his outrageous salary, "We make a lot, but we spend a lot." The same is true in the other directions. People lose jobs, take pay cuts, or have one parent leave the work force to stay at home and they get by. Sure, they have less stuff and spend less on entertainment. When many months pass, they ask themselves where all the money went before. When we are forced to tighten our belts, we are able to get buy.

Paying yourself first is very easy. The first thing you do every month before you do anything else, is put money away for retirement. So you are doing just what the name implies. You are paying yourself first. For the first few months this might be hard. Two hundred and fifty dollars (or however much you decide to invest) is a big deal to cut from a budget, but in a few months you won't even miss it.

There are lots of theories on how much money you should invest for retirement. Somewhere around ten percent of your income is a good place to start. I understand that ten percent is a lot of money, especially if you haven't been saving up to this point. I don't want to scare you off. Don't think, that is impossible, and just walk away. As we just saw, it is more important when you start than how much you save. If paying yourself first at ten percent seems unmanageable, work your way up to ten percent.

Let's assume you make thirty six thousand dollars a year. Instead of trying to find a way to cut three hundred dollars out of your budget, which is 10% of your income, start small with one percent. So instead of trying to live with out three hundred dollars, you are living with out thirty. That is reasonable. That could be skipping eating out once or twice a month. Live without that one percent for two months. In two months, you won't even notice the thirty dollars is gone. In month number three, pay yourself first–two percent. You have already learned how to live without the first thirty dollars, so now you are only learning how to live without thirty dollars. If you do this every two months in about a year and half you will be putting away ten percent of your income. Yes, this will take a sacrifice, but if you make this sacrifice now, as you have seen, it will pay off in the long term. Every time you are faced with a choice about how you are going to use your money (or time) and you are conflicted about the sacrifice you need to make recall the mental image of the life you can live with passion. It might be hard to live without thirty more dollars this month, but is it worth it for a life you can live with passion? Keep reminding yourself of what the goal is. It will make it easier to understand the sacrifice you facing and give you the strength to make it.

How to Invest

When I pick up a how-to-book of any sort, I like to dive right in. There is something I am trying to learn. I will admit, I can be a little (read a lot) impatient. I want to know what the author is offering right now. I will start with the beginning of the book, but if the introduction is nothing more than pages and pages of "thanks you's" by the author, I am inclined to skim (or skip the whole thing all together). It is not that I don't care how happy the author is with his hairdresser. I know everyone has family. But, that isn't why I picked up the book. I picked it up to learn. I want to learn. NOW!

With that being said, I would be willing to bet you are not much different from me. You wanted to get started right away, and I don't blame you. Since this might be the case I would like to reprint the "Disclaimer" from the front of this book which you might have skipped:

"PLEASE UNDERSTAND THAT PRESENTATION OF ANY PERFORMANCE DATA IS NOT MEANT TO IMPLY THAT SIMILAR RESULTS WILL BE ACHIEVED IN THE FUTURE. RATHER, PAST PERFORMANCE IS NO INDICATION OF FUTURE RESULTS AND ANY ASSERTION TO THE CONTRARY IS A FEDERAL OFFENSE. THE DATA IS PROVIDED MERELY FOR ILLUSTRA-TIVE AND DISCUSSION PURPOSES. PERFORMANCE DATA USING A WIDE VARIETY OF TIME PERIODS IS PROVIDED. RATHER THAN FOCUSING ON THE SPECIFIC TIME PERIODS USED OR THE RESULTS DERIVED, THE READER SHOULD FOCUS INSTEAD ON THE UNDERLYING PRINCIPLES.

"UNDERSTAND THAT NONE OF THE MATERIAL PRESENTED HERE IS INTENDED TO SERVE AS THE BASIS FOR ANY FINANCIAL DECISION, NOR DOES ANY OF THE INFORMA-TION CONTAINED WITHIN CONSTITUTE AN OFFER TO BUY OR SELL ANY SECURITY. SUCH AN OFFER IS MADE ONLY BY PROSPECTUS, WHICH YOU SHOULD READ CAREFULLY BEFORE INVESTING OR SENDING MONEY.

"UNDERSTAND THAT THE MATERIAL PRESENTED IS ACCURATE TO THE BEST OF OUR KNOWLEDGE. HOWEVER, PERFORMANCE DATA CHANGES OVER TIME, AND LAWS FREQUENTLY CHANGE AS WELL, AND MY ADVICE COULD CHANGE ACCORDINGLY. THEREFORE, THE READER IS ENCOURAGED TO VERIFY THE STATUS OF SUCH INFORMA-TION BEFORE ACTING."

I am not reprinting this section because my lawyer thought it would be a good idea. I reprinted it because there is some very important information contained within these statements that you need to understand when it comes times to invest your money. Let's take a look at what I think is the most important sentence of the entire Disclaimer. "Rather, past performance is no indication of future results and any assertion to the contrary is a federal offense."

I have already showed you the power of compound interest. I made statements like, "If you invest x dollars for 10 years at 10% you will end up with y dollars." That is completely true. It is possible to invest your money in a way that will do just this. But, *please read this carefully*, I don't want to mislead you to believe there is a category of investments out there called *10% returners*. Almost any personal finance literature that you will read will discuss the fact that over the long term the United States stock market has returned 10%. Over the long term. When we talk about long term in this context, we are talking about over the past 90 years. It is possible that in any given time the stock market will do much better than this (see 1998-99). It is also possible for the stock market to return much less even losing money over a period of time (see 2002). When you see financial advice that says the stock market should return 10%, in reality it says: "Over the long term, with ups and down, on average the stock market has returned 10%. Based on this data, we believe over the long term the marker will continue to return 10%". This is a statement of long term averages. It is saying, nothing is a sure thing. If it was a sure thing, then everyone would be doing it, and you wouldn't be reading this book.* Some people make money in the market and other loose money. What we need to do when we invest, is to do it in such a fashion that we are meeting our long term goals. There three are basic lessons that we can take from this:

INVEST FOR THE LONG TERM Since the data we are using to make our investment decisions is based on long term data, the only reasonable conclusions we can draw are for the long term. For example, let's say you are going on vacation to Italy this summer. You have never been to Italy. You figured out your itinerary. You have your passport. You have called your bank to let them know you will be using your ATM in a foreign country, so they don't think your card has been stolen. You eased your mother's concerns that you are going to be safe and come home in one piece. The last task is to pack your bags, but what to bring? One of the pieces of information you need is what the weather is like for this time of year in Italy. You can get your data two ways. You could look to see what the weather was like last year at this time or you could look at the historical averages to see what the weather is like. Obviously, the second set of data is much more useful. Last year, it might have been an unusual year. For some reason it was 15 degrees hotter. This year when it returns to the average, you will be underdressed. This is not to say that every year the temperatures will be found within the averages, but more than likely it will. Weather changes from year to year, but not too much. If you pack for weather within the average and bring an extra set of clothing for extraordinary stagnations, you will be fine.

Investing your money is no different. We have a set of historical data that lets us know what will probably happen. Even though this is the average, it doesn't mean this is what will happen each and every year. There are good and bad years in the market. If you build your investment strategy for the long term, you will ride out these ups and downs. The more time we have to reach our financial goals, the more likely we will reach them. That is a completely intuitive statement for any goal. If the goal you have is to be able to play FREEBIRD on the electric guitar, it will be an easier goal if you have six months to do it, verses six weeks. That is why it is so important to start working toward your financial goals right now. The sooner you start, the more time you will have to get where you want.

UNDERSTAND YOUR LEVEL OF RISK AVERSION There are many types of investments. There are stocks, bonds, gold, t-bills, foreign, domestic, small cap, big cap, saving account, and many more. Right now, it is not important to understand each of these types of investments. That will come with time. The important point right now is to

---

* Whenever you are researching an investment and it seems like a sure thing, it is probably not. If it seems too good to be to true, it probably is.

understand that each type of investment has a basic characteristic of possible risk and possible returns. In most cases, the higher the possible return, the higher the risk, and the lower the possible return, the lower the risk. This may seem obvious, but let's look at two examples to make sure we are on the same page.

High Risk/High Reward: In your research you encounter a small bio-tech company called Bill's Bio-Tech. They are doing research into creating single cell computers. Their plan is to take a single cell and engineer it in a way that it can hold a single piece of data. The cells are combined to create computer memory. Because they can create storage at the cellular level, they believe that on a single piece of memory, the size of a postage stamp, they will be able to hold a whole library of data. It is a very exciting company, but at this point they still have a few hurdles to get over. First, they are only able to connect a hundred cells to make memory. At this point a few hundred cells is not useful because it can't do much. Second, because they are still developing the technology, they have no cheap way of mass-producing it. Right now it takes a team of three scientists a week to make one piece of memory. The up side of this investment is obvious. If they are able to bring this product to market, it will completely transform technology. Imagine having a whole library nof data on your cell phone. If they meet their goals the company could be worth billions of dollars. On the other hand, it is still not know if they will be able to make the technology work on a large scale. Also, if they do get over this hurdle, there is no way to know if they will be able to stream line the production to produce memory in a cheap fashion. It does the market place no good to create a piece of memory that costs a million dollars. If they don't solve these problems, an investor would lose their whole investment. There is the possibility of high reward with this investment, but there is also very high risk.

Low Risk/Low Reward: The most basic of low risk/low reward investment is a savings account. With a savings account, the bank guarantees a monthly return. For example, two percent over the course of a year. With the rate of return, it will take a very long time for this money to grow in a meaningful fashion. On the other hand, there is only one way you could lose your money. First, the bank would have to go bankrupt. Banks are required to have insurance for such situation. If a bank went out of business, the insurance provider would return your money. In the case of a bank, that insurer is the federal government. The only way you will lose your money in this investment is to have your bank and the federal government go under. If the federal government goes under, you will have much bigger problems than losing your savings. Here there is a very low return, but also very low risk.

Every investment you make is going to have a different set of risk/reward variables. What you base your investment decisions on is two basic factors. The first is what your financial goals are. For example, Jack and Jill both need $700,000 to retire. They both have the same amount of money to invest each month in retirement. The difference is Jill is 25 and Jack 45. Because Jill has much more time to reach her goals, she will be able to invest in a riskier manner because she has more time to recover from down turns. The second factor to understand is your level of *risk aversion*. The simplest definition of a risk aversion level, is how much risk you can handle before you start losing sleep over choices. This is a matter of disposition. Just like when we talked about creating your long term emergency fund. Two people could be in the exact same situation. Same income. Same size of family. Same monthly expenses. It is possible that person one needs a six month emergency fund to sleep soundly at night, while the other only needs four months of savings to get to bed at night. The same factors come into play when you're investing for retirement. Because of our disposition, some of us will be more comfortable with more risk than others. This is your money and your future. You need to be comfortable with your choices. You need to balance your financial goals with your ability to tolerate risk.

If you are starting later in life, it is possible that you might run into a problem. It is conceivable that you are just starting to save for your retirement at 55, and you want to retire at 65. This means you only have 10 years to reach your goals. At the same time, you are a person who is very risk adverse (have a low tolerance for risk). You are only comfortable in low risk investments, but need to find high reward investments because of the short time frame. This will not happen. Either you need to re-evaluate your goals or you need to tolerate more risk. More than likely the second will not happen. We can educate ourselves to understand what the rational level of risk is in an investment, but I am yet to meet a person who could change how much risk they can tolerate. This is very much part of our make up. In the end, this means you need to change your financial plan. Maybe you will live on less. Maybe you will decide to retire later. Maybe you will pick up a second job to make a little more money so you can invest in a less risky manner. What you can't do is assume it is just going to work out. It does you no good to follow a plan that will not work. That is just foolish.

INVEST IN A WAY THAT WILL INSULATE YOU FROM LARGE MARKET FLUCTUATIONS It is a given that the market will go up and down. If we were really smart, we would make sure that we sell right before the market went down, and bought right before it went up. There is no sure fire way to do that. Even professionals, who work with the market full time, can't do this all the time.

The other important fact to note is that the whole market doesn't move together. Even if you have no experience investing, I am willing to bet you recognize the term the Dow Jones Industrial Average. I don't expect you to know exactly what it is. You know they talk about it all the time on the news and you know enough that when it goes up–it is probably good and when it goes down–it is probably bad. Let's take a close look at the Dow to illustrate the fact that the market doesn't always move in one direction.

The Dow is nothing more than the combined value of 30 very large companies. So at the end of the day if Dow is up 40 points it means all 30 companies combined are up 40 points. For example if IBM was up 10, GE was down 5, and no other stock moved for the day then the Dow would be up 5. Generally speaking if the Dow is up for the day, more than likely it means more companies were up than down. If the Dow has gone down, then the converse is probably true. The
important lesson for us is that the market does not move in a uniform fashion. This makes sense. Just because technology is down doesn't necessarily mean health care is down as well. Don't get bogged down in the details of the Dow right now. The important that take away is that not all investments move in the same direction at the same time.

If you have been paying attention, you will notice that we have just introduced one more variable that we need to worry about. Not only do we have to pay attention to the market moving up and down, we also have to be aware that different types of investments will be moving in different directions. This can seem very overwhelming. Fear not. We have another tool in our arsenal to deal with just this fact: diversification. To put it in layman's terms, "Don't keep all your eggs in one basket." The way to deal with different sectors moving in different ways, is to invest in a number of them. (The term "sector" can refer to different types of investments, such as stock and bonds, or different types of investments in one area, technology stocks vs. healthcare.) If we invest in both healthcare and tech, we can benefit from both when they are moving up. This doesn't mean you can buy any tech stock and any healthcare stock and be okay. You still need to carefully select each investment. Only then can diversification be a useful and powerful tool.

Here is a real world example of what can happen if you don't diversify. It comes from our friends at Enron. I am sure you are aware of some of the details of the Enron fiasco. One of the biggest parts of the story surrounds the number of people who lost everything when the company, and its stock price, collapsed. In no way am I going to exonerate the actions of Enron's management. It is becoming quite clear that not only did they make some very poor choices, but they also probably broke a number of laws.* These actions lead directly to the collapse of the company. This does not mean the employees that lost so much escape blame.

As part of their compensation, the employees received stock. As time past this stock went up and up. On paper, there were many millionaires working at Enron. The mistake the employees made (and it is a mistake that falls squarely on their shoulders) was they did not diversify. The stock kept going up. I am sure they felt like they were just minting money. Then one day it all went away as did all their savings. It seemed too good to be true *because it was*. They were not hurt by a major market down turn, but the collapse of one company. The smart employees would have sold Enron stock along the way and diversified to protect themselves. Sure they wouldn't have had a value growing like those who owned lots of Enron, but today, they would also have money.

THE TAKE AWAY IS THIS: The best way to fight large fluctuations in the market, is to insulate yourself from the risk of having one investment hurt you too much. You do this by investing in many different sectors. Simple enough, right? But this is much more than a question of what I should do. It doesn't do you any good to simply know what the right thing is to do, you must also know how to do it. Just relax, this is something you are capable of doing and it won't consume all your time. One of the easiest ways of doing this, is to invest in mutual funds, which is a topic we will get to next.

Where to Invest: Mutual Funds

NOTE: It is important to point out, this is not the definitive personal finance book. This book does not contain all the information you are going to need for your financial success. This is only the start. The goal here is to get you going down the right road. As you get more control over your personal finances you will need to continue to educate yourself. Mutual funds are probably the easiest and most convenient way to invest. This does not mean it is the only or best way to invest. As your savings grow over time, you are going to want to consider other types of investments.

Mutual funds are simple. A mutual fund is nothing more than a collection of investments that have a manager which you can buy a part of. A mutual fund can have stocks, bonds, currency, or real-estate. Basically, the way the fund works is there is a fund manager. The fund manager can be a single person or a company. In most cases, the fund is run by a company, which then assigns one person to

*At the time of this printing, litigation was still pending.

manager the fund. Individual investors contribute to the fund. The fund manager then invests the money. Investor A could contribute $100 while investor B could contribute $100,000. The fund manager then invests the money. The individual investors do as well or as poorly as the whole fund.

A mutual fund can be as small as a few million dollars or as big as billions of dollars. Some funds only invest in one type of investment while others are greatly diversified. In the United States alone there are thousands of mutual funds. Mutual funds are nothing more than an investment tool. They are not a particular type of investment, but instead a way to invest. You are not more likely to earn or lose money in a mutual fund.

If there is nothing really different about mutual funds *Why choose mutual funds?* There are three two reasons for mutual funds. First, they are easy to invest in. In most cases you can set up an account with whichever fund (or funds) you are going to invest in and simply write a check when you are ready to invest. Most fund let you invest at anytime. You will receive regular accounting for how the fund is doing, much like a bank statement, so it is very easy to keep records. Second, it takes very little money to get into a mutual fund. If you wanted to buy stock you must have enough money to buy in full shares. For example, if you wanted to buy stock in Bill's Bio Tech and the shares are worth $100. You could only buy whole shares of stock. It would be very difficult to diversify in this circumstance. On the other hand, with a mutual fund, you can invest any amount. Let's say you are investing in Fund ABC which has a market value of $1,000,000 (meaning all of its holds value adds up to $1,000,000). If you invest $100 in this fund, then you would own 1/10,000 the fund. You would also own a small portion of every single holding in the fund. This allows you to diversify your investments and still only invest a small amount of money.

The next obvious question is *Which fund or funds to choose?* I don't have a good answer for that because you will need to pick a fund that meets your investing needs. Like every investment (because a mutual fund is nothing more than a collection of investments) every mutual fund has its own characteristics. Each fund will have its own set of possible risks and possible rewards. There are funds that only invest in government funds which are safe but have low return, while others only invest in high risk foreign companies. You are going to need to find a fund that meets your needs. When you do choose a fund, there are a number of factors to consider.

KNOW WHAT YOU ARE BUYING It is very important that you do your research before you choose where to invest. When choosing a fund, look at the past history of the fund. Don't just look at the last six months or a year. Look over the last five to ten years. This will give you much more historical data about the fund. Every bookstore has tons of books on mutual funds. Pick up MONEY magazine. Read the finance section of USATODAY. Do your research. This is not complicated, but it is important you know what you are doing.

KNOW WHO THE FUND MANAGER IS Make sure that the current fund manager is the same person who was managing the fund while the past results were manufactured. It is possible for fund managers to move on. It is important you know who is controlling the money.

KEEP AN EYE ON COMMISSIONS There is going to be a fee charged for every transaction you make. Know how much you are paying for each transaction. If it is costing you $9 dollars every time you make a purchase and you are investing $300 then you have already lost 1% with out the fund moving. If you have less than $50,000 is savings then you should only be investing in no load mututal funds, which means there is a service fee, but there is no few to buy or sell shares.

DON'T BE AFRAID TO GET OUT It is possible that you have made a bad choice. Don't be afraid to get out of the bad choice before it becomes a horrible choice. Cash out a bad investment while there is still some value. It is okay to move on.

REINVEST THE DIVIDEND There are two ways that an investment gains value. First, the value of the investment (such as a stock) goes up. This means you will be able to sell it for more than you bought it. The second way an investment can gain value, is by paying out a dividend. A dividend is nothing more than your share of the profit as the part owner (your shares) of a company. For example, I own stock in a small bank and twice a year I receive a dividend check of one to two dollars a share. In order to take advantage of the dividend in a real way, over the long haul, is to reinvest the dividend. It is possible to automatically re-invest the dividend. This simply means, instead of them sending you a check, they simply buy more shares.

When to Invest: Dollar Averaging

We have all heard the simple investing advice, "buy low and sell high." Piece of cake, right? I know for a fact that I am not smart enough to beat the market. It requires research, time, and luck. So what are we common folk supposed to do? It is actually much easier than you would think. The way to do it is called "dollar averaging". Dollar averaging is not illegal, and it is not a big secret. Almost every personal finance book will talk about the technique.

The reason that dollar averaging works is because over a long period of time historically the stock market goes up. [Remember: Past performance does not imply similar performance will happen in the future.] Dollar averaging is investing in such a way, it forces you to buy less when prices are high and more when prices are low. It works like this. Let's assume that each month you have $100 to invest. You decide that each month you are going to buy Mutual Fund ACF. In January, the fund is valued at $10 a share so you buy 10 shares. In February ACF takes a dive and is now valued at $5 a share, so you buy 20 shares with your $100. In March, ACF makes a modest recovery to the value of $7.50. This month with your $100 you are able to buy 15 shares of stock. There are two things that might strike you at this point. First of all dollar averaging isn't very sexy. You might be thinking, "When I am hanging out with my friends, I can't tell them about the exciting stock moves I made." You are correct. Dollar averaging is very boring. If you want exciting, go bungee jumping. Your second thought is, "This dollar averaging thing isn't so great, I am only three months into the process and all ready I own a loser." You are wrong.

Let's take a look at what has happened to ACF so far. You have now purchased 45 shares (10 in Jan., 20 in Feb. and 15 in March) of the fund at a cost to you of $300. Right now the fund is worth $7.50 a share, meaning your shares are now worth $337.50. The stock is worth 25% less than when you first bought, and you have made more than 10% on the investment. How did that happen? Very simply, you bought more when the price was low (20 shares at $5) and bought less when the price was high (10 shares at $10). This way you don't have to outsmart the market. It averages out, assuming you are investing in fund that is going up over the long term. This doesn't work if the fund goes down in value every month. For this to work, you must have an investment that is going up over the long term. I will admit that the example I have given here is more dramatic than what the market normally. Very rarely has there been 50% swings in one month, but it does illustrate the point. Assuming the market over the long term keeps going up, dollar averaging will insure you buy the right amount at the right time.

Ethical Investing

There are a number of factors to consider when investing your money, as we have just talked about. You need to consider what your short and long term goals are. You need to understand your level of risk. Before you decide where you invest, there is one final factor that I think it is important to consider. You need to decide what types of companies you want to invest in. I am not talking about sector or size of the companies. I am talking about, "What are the values the company the holds?" The current term of art for this factor is *ethical investing*.

I truly believe we articulate who we are by the choices we make. How we use our money, in every way, is no different. Ethical investing is nothing more than making sure that our investments line up with our belief system. There are no hard and fast rules for ethical investing, because the values that "ethical" investors hold are different from investor to investor. For example, alcohol and tobacco stocks are very profitable, but are you comfortable making money off of these products? That is a question you need to answer for yourself. In the world of mergers, acquisitions, and behemoth companies, it becomes even more complicated. Let's look at an example.

You decided that you do not want to invest in any tobacco companies. You are doing all the homework that you are suppose to do. After a few weeks of research, you have decided to consider making an investment into Mutual Fund APX. In your research, you have discovered the fund has a good history of return, the fund manager who has had the past success is still the fund manager, and the level of risk is in line with yours. Your last step is to make sure the fund meets your ethical investing standards. For this example, we will assume your only issue is not wanting to invest in companies that produce tobacco products. You look through the companies that are listed in the mutual fund and there are no tobacco companies. Great, time to invest. Right? Maybe not. Would you feel comfortable investing in RJR Nabisco? I mean, who doesn't love crackers? And as a stock they have had a decent track record, right? Well in the 1990's RJR Nabisco owned the companies that produced the Philip Morris brand cigarettes. Because of pressure of the tobacco law suits in 1999, the Nabisco foods we spun out into own food only company.

I can hear you thinking, "Great! This is even more research that I need to do. Not only do I need to research the funds, I also have to research each company." Or more likely you might be thinking, "This is just too much work! I give up." Have faith, the free market to the rescue! Over the past ten years as more and more private investors (folks like you and me) have not only entered the market place, but they are also taking much more care in how they choose to invest. With greater global awareness, more people are trying to invest ethically. Because of this, fund managers understand they are more likely to have people invest in their fund if the fund matches the social conscious of possible investors. In plain English: The buyers want investments they are comfortable in. The funds want to sell their services, so they sell what the buyer wants, ethical investing funds.

The way a fund manager meets the needs of an ethical investor is by creating something very simple called a screen. A screen is nothing more than criteria that "screens" out what the investor doesn't want. For example, a tobacco screen would eliminate investing in any company that has any tobacco holdings at all (like RJR Nabisco in the 80's and 90's). There are many types of screens. There are screens for tobacco, alcohol, sweat (no companies that use sweat labor), green (only companies that meet a high environmental standard), and many more.

I am being honest; there are a number of very enticing investments which will fail under the weight of screens. That doesn't mean that you are limited to low return on your investment. There are lots of wonderful (profitable) companies out there. You will need to do a little more research. In my mind, in the end, this extra work is well worth it, because you know that your money is working in the market place in a way that is in line with what you believe.

BUYING STUFF

The analogy continues...We have gotten out of the rain. The holes have been plugged, the foundation is secure and you are starting to work on the long term. You need to think of the day-to-day maintenance and filling the house with furniture. We simply can't save for the future; we also live in the moment. So, for a moment, let's talk about our buying habits and how they can contribute to our financial health.

Keeping up with the Jones

Why did the monkey fall out of the tree? It was dead. Why did the second monkey fall out of the tree? It was stapled to the first. Why did the third monkey fall out of the tree? Peer pressure.

Over and over again we warn children about the ills of peer pressure. Peer pressure does not go away after we go to prom and stop having acne. We all want to feel successful, and it is easy to get caught up in the American dream of owning a home with a white picket fence or a really cool urban row house, a new car every few years, and 2.7 kids. Sometimes it is very vocal pressure. For example, your parents nagging you to be working someplace that pays more or to start having grandkids. Other times the pressure is unspoken, in the way everyone dresses around you.

In their book THE MILLIONAIRE NEXT DOOR Thomas J. Stanley and William D. Danko point to the characteristics which are common for most millionaires in the US (a group most of us would like to be a part of). The facts they found were very interesting. Most millionaires own their own homes, but they are not extravagant. They own cars that are on the average of two year old (or older). They are not working high paingy jobs. What they also point out that is equally interesting, is the number of people who make high dollar (more than $75,000 a year) who are not millionaires. The reason being, in most cases, they are spending what they make. Just because they are making more doesn't mean they are any more disciplined than you or I when it comes to savings. They have opulent homes (or more house than they need), they always have new cars, more new clothes than they need, and very expensive watches. They have fallen prey to making more which means you should have more.

You need to stop comparing yourself to those around you. This can be even more dangerous if you are working in a lower paying field such as teaching, ministry, or social work. Most of your friends are not going to be living on the same salary as you. Trying to keep up can become an issue of self worth. The cars they drive, the clothes they wear, and the places they go out to eat. You can't give into the pressure. You must decide that living a life with passion, is more important than fitting in. You have no idea if the people you are trying to keep up with are on their way to financial ruin. It is your job to make sure that you are not on that road. Peer presure is hard to recognize. You need to make sure you are making your choices based off of the life you want to live, not so you have some cool story to tell your fiends over dinner next week of the super cool stereo you just bought.

Taking Your Time

I own a XM satellite radio. Basically, it the equivalent of a TV dish for my radio. Two of my favorite stations to listen to are the comedy channels. They are 24 hours a day of stand up comedy. In one of Margaret Smith's bits I heard recently, she was talking about how much grief she received when she returned a blouse. When she was pressed by the very snotty clerk why she was bringing the garment back, she said, "I got home and realized I liked the song that was playing when I was in store, not the blouse."

You should only make purchases that you need. It is okay to need a new pair of shoes, if it fits into your total plan. My sister's husband will take three days to buy a pair of running shoes, and this is after he has found the pair he wants. This might seem a little extreme, but it serves as a good model. You should wait at least three days between deciding to make a major purchase and actually making the purchase. I would call a major purchase anything over $75.

Shopping is an intoxicating endeavor. It is all about you. Hunting for something you want, be it a new pair of shoes, or a big screen TV. Finding it. Then bringing it home. Being able to answer the question, "What did you do today?" with, "I bought these great shoes. I can't wait to show you!" Think of all the really cool things you have bought that are now gathering dust, or not as great as you thought at first. If you take the time to really think about a purchase, you will be able to tell the difference between want and need.

Take It Back

You had a moment of weakness and bought something you really don't need (or even want for that matter). You can beat yourself up about the purchase and fear how much your spouse is going kill you, or you can do the right thing: take it back. Sure, you will have to swallow your pride, admitting you are wrong. More than likely, you will get grief from the clerks at the store. Get over it. Suck it up. Raise your right hand and say, "I made a mistake." Then fix the mistake, by taking it back. Even if the store charges a 10% restock fee. A 10% stupid penalty is better than a 100% stupid penalty.

Saving Money

What if I told you that in the next hour you could make $100? I have your attention. Yes? I am not talking about some get quick rich ploy or pyramid scheme (excuse me, multi level marketing). I am talking about a simple way you can make money or at least doing something that has the same effect as making money. I am talking about saving money. I am not talking about clipping coupons. Many times coupons cause you to spend more because you buy items or brands that you normally wouldn't. I am talking about shopping around.

Not only should you take time to decide that you are buying something you really want, but make sure that you are getting the best price. Let's take for an example you are looking to buy a new TV. After a lot of research you decide that you want a 24" TV made by Apex with a built-in DVD player. You have also taken the three to five days of thinking, to decide that, at this time, you can afford it and it something the whole family can agree on. Your job is to get the best deal. Take one hour and make phone calls to all the places in your town that sells TVs. Quickly ask them if they have the product you want and how much it is. Also, don't be afraid to play one retailer off another. Many major chains guarantee that they will beat any price. Also, go online and search to find a better deal. There are a number of sites which do a price comparison for you.*

Bargain

When I travel, I learn things about myself I never dreamed would be true. I was in an artist market in Ecuador, when I learned I was really good at bargaining.

---

* Remember what your grandmother said, "If the deal is too good to be true, it probably is." If you find any electronic online for considerably less then likely one of two things are true. Either one, it is not new, but refurbished, or two, grey market. Grey market means the product has been imported into the country in a fashion that is not supported by the manufacturer. In these cases the warranty will be null and void.

Even in a language I barely spoke. I was so good at it that one of the locals, who was traveling with us, had me go in and bargain for a bag she wanted for her daughter. I realized very quickly, the reason that I am good at bargaining was I understood the value I placed on the object I wanted. It has nothing to do with what others were paying for the item, or what people normally pay for it. All that matters is what it was worth to me. When I negotiate, I go back and forth with the person until I get to my price. If they aren't willing to come to my price, I don't buy the item. It requires me to not get emotionally attached to the item. I also have to get over the feeling of feeling bad for not buying something. But, why pay more for something than it is worth to you?

When I got back to the States, I realized this was really a good plan of attack when I bought everything. Let's take pants for an example. I have a general rule that I should never spend more than $20 on a regular pair of pants and I should really shoot for $10. I have come to this price because I have found lots of really great pants on clearance racks and outlet stores for that price. These are not the trendiest pants in the world, but they are just pants. Their job is to cover my legs, stay up, and match my shirt. That is what pants are worth to me.

Let's pretend I have found these great pants that I love (well, as much as I can love a pair of pants) and they are $30. Originally I would say, "These are great pants, but they are not worth $30 to me." I would leave the store emptyhanded. I was staying within my clothing budget, but there were a few things I was regretting I didn't have. I wasn't losing sleep over it, because I was only spending what I thought the things were worth, but there must be another way. Then it struck me. Why not bargain? The next time I found this great shirt on a sale rack that was out of my price range, I asked to see the manager for a deal. I said, "This is a really great shirt, but it is only worth $20 to me. Can I have it for $20?" The manager said no, but he was willing take another 20%. It was still too much for me. I didn't buy the shirt, but it emboldened me to realize it is okay to bargain. If the store was offended by my offer, I would take my business somewhere else. They want me as customer. They want to sell stuff. On their end, the shirt has a particular value. They are obviously not going to give me the shirt for $1, but there might be some middle ground. I now use the practice all the time for clothing. It only works occasionally, but I never pay more than what I think something is worth.

Barter

You don't have to buy everything–you can trade. Think of all the unique things you have to offer. There is someone in this world that needs your giftedness. Don't be afraid to turn to friends and neighbors and offer a trade. Baby-sit their kids to get some help on your taxes. Clean their gutter to get your oil changed.

I know bartering seems foolish, some system from a bygone time. The questions is this: Would you rather a) live a life with passion or b) not look silly to your friends? If they are your friends, they won't laugh at you, at least not to your face. This is not about them, it is about you. Just look at the life you want to live. It is okay to get creative in reaching your goals.

Cars

It is the amazing the love affair we Americans have with driving. I believe it is one of the ways we, as a culture, express our sense of individual freedom. To have the ability to go anywhere we want at a moments notice is liberating. I can still remember the first time I was allowed to drive somewhere by myself. It was the same day I passed my driving test. I was able to talk my mother into letting me pick my sister up from practice. I am the oldest. Being the first child to drive, it took a little work to convince my mother that "the government trusts me to drive, so should you." In retrospect, I am not sure if that is the soundest reasoning, but it worked. So I climbed into a 72 Buick Skylark my parents had bought for $250 dollars. I was free, and I haven't looked back. I love to drive and hate being a passenger.

The first time I went to Iceland, I was struck by the types of cars I encountered. Basically, every car fit into two categories. They were either so small that if you couldn't find a parking spot you simply put the car in your back pocket, or they had tires that were at least three feet tall to get over the snow and ice on the glaciers. The cars were built functionally–small to use very little gas or big to get through the elements. Even looking at a number of the small cars made by three different manufacturers, they were all about the same design. There was no real style. Nothing like the US car market.

Cars (and growing up in Wyoming–trucks) are more than a mode of transportation. They say something about us. People buy sports cars that can go 180 mph, but they have never driven faster than 10 miles over the speed limit. People buy SUVs and Hummers, but the most treacherous driving they do is trying to find a parking spot they can fit into at the mall. But, it all makes sense. We love our cars. We love how powerful they make us feel. Most of us are far past being hip and cool. I can still remember the day I realized that I just couldn't keep dying my hair blue. Blue hair was very cool, but I was not. For some reason, once all other fashion has reasonably passed us by, we still feel comfortable in a cool car. Sometimes, it even empowers us to have a sense of cool we have not had in a long time.

My advice is to buy the car you need, not the car you want. When it comes time to buy your next car, think functionality, not fun. I am not suggesting you get some box on wheels with just an AM radio. If you have three kids under the age of 8, getting the minivan with the build-in TV/VCR might be a necessity. That is functionality. The automatic seat warmers serve a function, but are they a function that you can live without? (The answer to that question is "yes.")

The next time you need to buy a car, think about what is the functionality you really need. How many people are normally going to be riding in the car? If it is you, your spouse and the kids, the two door just won't cut it. Do you have a need to haul large things regularly? If you only need to haul big things from time to time, there is no reason to get a big SUV. Sure it is nice to decide to get rid of the couch in the front room at a moment's notice, but if you are only hauling things two or three times a year, it makes more sense to borrow a friend's vehicle. Bigger vehicles get worse gas mileage. When you are driving around with the space empty you are just wasting money on gas. It is less convenient not to own the vehicle, but will be worth it in the long run. It is important not to buy more vehicle than you really need.

Second, you should buy a used vehicle. Cars lose up to 60% of their value in four years, and as much as 20% the day you drive it off the lot. That is a bad investment. It is not as much fun as buying a brand new car that has new car smell, but financially it makes more sense. You don't have to go out and buy a 1982 Yugo when you are buying a used car. If you do your homework, you will be able to find many used cars that are only a year or two old. People with more money than you or I (or no sense of their money), trade in practically new cars all the time for such reasons as they no longer like the color. These vehicles are in great shape. Many are still under the manufacturer's warranty and they cost much less than a new car. If the car only has a short amount of time (or no time) left on the manufacturer's warranty it is possible to purchase an extended warranty. Also, buy the car from someone you trust. You might be able to save a few bucks by buying a car out of the classifieds, but I would recommend going to a dealership which has a used car department. If something goes dramatically wrong you will know where to find the seller.

Third, pay cash for your car. It is this great misconception that we must be paying a car payment. So much so, the instance we pay off one car we see it as a sign it is time to trade it in and get a new one. It is hard work to save money and pay cash for a car, but this isn't about doing what is easy, it is about doing what is best for your financial future. Any debt that you have will keep you from moving towards your saving goals. Save the money for a car. Pay cash, not only will you feel better, it makes better financial sense.

Also, consider buying a car with good gas mileage. It may not seem like a big deal to get a car that gets a few more miles to the gallon, but over the life of the car it will add up to savings. Look at three cars which get 20, 25, and 30 miles to the gallon respectively. Assuming your drive 20,000 miles a year and gas cost $1.80 a gallon. You would spend $1800, $1440, and $1200 a year on gas respectively. Getting five extra miles to the gallon would save you $360 a year or $1800 if you owned the car for five years. Getting 10 extra miles to the gallon would save you $600 a year and $3000 over the five year life of the car.

Finally, regardless of the car you buy, you need to do your homework. There is so much information now available. Once you decide the make, model, and year of the car you want, you can easily check prices with every dealership within hundreds of miles of you online.

Gift Giving: Consumable, Home Made, or Donations

I had a rough time Christmas shopping last year. The year before was much easier. I spent a month studying Spanish in Ecuador. Even though I was there in August, I had Christmas on the mind. The whole time I was in Ecuador I carried a list of all the people I wanted to shop for. Not only did I look for cool gifts, I wanted to find just the right gift for each person. It was lots of fun. It was a reason to think about my loved ones. I tried to put as much care and thought into each gift. Last year, on the other hand, was no good.

I found myself standing in some department store a week before Christmas, just staring at the racks and racks of DVDs. I figured DVDs were innocuous enough. Try and find something they would like. I ended up not buying things they would buy, but probably things they would rent. It was horrifying. Buying gifts because that is what we do. The love of the season, right? It was pathetic. I was pathetic. The problem stems from the fact we don't need stuff. All of my family–we just don't need stuff. Of the three children, my sister is the youngest at 25. We all have established lives. I am the only one in my family who doesn't own a home. We don't need more stuff. But gift giving turns into trying to find stuff for someone else. Stuff they probably don't need.

I am not suggesting we need to get rid of the whole gift-giving phenomena. Giving gifts is a way to show love, but there are other, better–and most of the time cheaper–ways of showing love. Recommendations I would have:

GIVE CONSUMABLE GIFTS Food and drink is always a great gift. Not only will they enjoy it, but many times you will as well. I would encourage you also to get creative with the gift of food. Not only give something good to eat (or drink), do it in a thoughtful manner. Once I gave a girl (I can call her a girl because I was a boy at the time) 774 HERSHEY'S KISSES ®, one for every day I knew her.

GIVE EXPERIENCES Send the ones you love to the movies, the theater, a concert or sky diving. Give them something that will not take up space, but will create a memory. As an added bounce, to people who have kids, offer to babysit.

MAKE AN IN KIND DONATION One of my favorite gifts of all time was a goat I received for my birthday. I didn't get the goat, but friends bought a family in need, a goat in my name. Find the cause that your loved ones are passionate about. Make a donation on their behalf. Do more than just send a check. Send a note to the organization explaining about the person for whom you are making the donation. Explain why their cause is important to your loved one. Make a card for your loved one explaining what you have done and include a copy of the note you sent, letting them know what you think of them. My sister and her husband took this idea one step further. Instead of giving some ridiculous (I mean very thoughtful) take away gift to everyone who came to their wedding, they made a small in-kind donation for everyone who attended. They spent the weeks leading up the wedding doing research to find just the right cause for each person. At the reception all of the name cards had on the inside, the charity in which a donation was made in their name. All the name cards were placed on a table by the door. As people entered the reception hall, they were able to see what charity the other guests were passionate about. When the bridesmaids saw the cards they cried (but they cried at everything that day).

GIVE SOMETHING HOMEMADE I don't care if you are not the creative type, make something for your loved ones. I know when someone has made something for me, I appreciate the time and effort they have put in. It means so much more than picking up something quick at the bookstore. If you are not the creative type, don't wimp out, find help. Also, if you are not creative and work really hard, it will be even more appreciated.

GIVE THEM SOMETHING THEY REALLY NEED A friend from high school got married last year. He and his bride registered at Wal-Mart. They registered for linens, appliances, and toilet paper. They registered for trash cans and windshield-wiper fluid. Even more fun than what they registered for was the fact people bought them those things. Most of the people who bought wacky home furnishings made sure everyone one noticed. My friend Nancy showed up with the largest container of toilet paper I have ever seen. It was unwrapped and had a big red bow on top. My friends had just bought a new house. They didn't need fine china. What they needed was a trash can. Give people things they really need. It might not be as much fun when they open it up, but in the long run it will get a lot more use.

HOME OWNERSHIP

I am not going to go into how to buy a home. That is a much bigger topic than this book, but I will share a few things I believe about homes and homeownership in the context of your financial plan. You might be surprised at what I have to say.

HOME IS A PLACE TO LIVE This is an idea I learned from personal finance guru Ric Edelman, which I think is right on. This statement runs counter to everything you have ever heard about homeownership. Let me say it again. A home might have some of the benefits of an investment, but it is not an investment. It is a place to live. With investments we are told to buy low and sell high, but home buying happens when we need a new home. The time you buy a new bigger home is when you no longer fit in your old home. The time you sell your home is when you move to another part of the country because you have a new job. Those events have nothing to do with the home market at the time you buy and sell. You buy and sell, for the most part, out of necessity. For example, you get transferred. The town you are currently living in has hit some hard times, so the entire real estate market is depressed. Because of this, your home is worth $30,000 less than when you bought it. But you can't wait for the market to rebound. You have to move, and you must sell now. There are financial benefits to homeownership, but if homeownership is your financial plan, you are in trouble.

NEVER GET A MORTGAGE LONGER THAN 15 YEARS Some would argue that you should pay cash for everything, even a home. Extreme? Yes. Most of us aren't going to be this zealous in our approach to money management. If you take out a mortgage, it should not be longer than 15 years. Let's look at the facts. Let's assume you get a mortgage for $120,000 at 7%. On a 30 year mortgage the payment is $798.36 a month. On a 15 year mortgage the payment is $1078.59. At first glance your thought is, "That is a $280 a month difference. I can't afford that." But look at the long term. On the 30 year mortgage your total payment will be $287,409.60 while the total payment on the 15 mortgage is only $194,146.20. That is the only time in my life I will say "only $194,146.20". For $280 a month, you save $93,263.40 in the long run, and you free up your mortgage payment to use for other things 15 years earlier. If you would like to see the difference between different mortgages check out WWW.MORTGAGE-CALC.COM.

"EVERYONE IS DOING IT," IS A BAD REASON TO BUY A HOME I understand the social pressures of having friends who are homeowners. When they buy, there is the housewarming party and housewarming gifts. When you get together to socialize, they share about the home improvement project they are working on. We are told over and over again, home ownership is part of the America dream. It is easy to feel inadequate when your peers are living "the American Dream" and you are not. Get over it. You are not your house, and you should only buy a house because it is the right decision for you.

IT IS A REALTORS AND MORTGAGE BROKER'S JOB TO SELL YOU STUFF Your realtor and mortgage broker might be the nicest people in the world. They might be the most honest people in the world, but they make their living by selling you a home and a mortgage. Once the home is sold, their jobs are done. From that point on, all of the risk is in the hands of the institution financing the mortgage. If a mortgage broker says you qualify for a certain loan, it doesn't mean it is a loan that you can afford. I am not saying that realtors and mortgage brokers are crooks, but their job is to help you live your dream, which is a big house and large yard. Just remember they are working on commission, the larger the home or mortgage, the higher their commission.

IF YOU CAN'T AFFORD THE PAYMENTS, YOU CAN'T AFFORD THE HOME If you have to do financial gymnastics with balloon payments, interest only payments, or variable interest rates then you can't afford the home. This is the largest personal purchase you will make in your life. Make sure you do it right. I would recommend not spending more that 30% of your income on a home payment. Yes, I might be conservative. If that is not manageable, am I saying "No, you shouldn't buy a home."? Not really. What I am saying is it is not a good idea to buy a home now.

CONSIDER YOUR LONG TERM GOALS WHEN BUYING A HOME Maybe you are in a situation where you have found the perfect home. It is in a great neighborhood. It is really close to your parents (or really far away, depending on your world view). You have done a good job of saving a down payment, and with your budget you can afford the payments on your 15 year fixed rate mortgage. It is time to buy the home, right? Well, there is at least one more thing to consider. What are your long term goals? You should ask this in terms of long term income. You are young, married, both you and your spouse have great jobs, and you have no kids. But, what does the future hold? What if you want kids? Is the plan to have both of you stay at work, or is one of you going to come home to become the primary care giver? If someone is quitting their job, you will be down one income. Take away one income. Can you still afford the added expense of an extra mouth (or three), all your other bills, and the house payment? Just something to consider.

NEVER BUY A CONDO You should never buy a condo, minus one situation. Condos are a bad idea for a number of reasons. Your property value is directly impacted by the other condos in your building. If someone else is letting their condo go to pot in your building, it will directly effect the value of your condo. Second, you are dependent on the condo association for the upkeep of the building. If they do that poorly, it also affects the value of your property. Third, there are always new condos being built. Why would you buy an older condo if you can have a new one? Old homes are "charming." They are "fixer uppers." An old condo is an old condo.

There is one exception to this rule. The only place it might be a good idea to buy a condo is in a urban neighborhood of a major city. In a major city, there is no room for new condos to be built. This will help maintain the value of a condo the same way it does with homes in a downtown area of a major city, assuming half the downtown population doesn't up and leave (see Baltimore in the 1980's).

It's Okay Not to Own a Home

You might argue that I am against homeownership. I am not. I think home ownership is a wonderful idea *for some people*. There is just so much sentiment in the world saying buying a home is always the right thing to do. I wanted to present the counterpoint before you get so excited about homeownership that you close your ears to the counterpoints. I believe there are a number of good reasons to rent.

YOU CAN LEAVE We live in a very mobile society. Some people change locations as fast as they change their cars or their hair styles. As a renter, if you have to leave immediately you might have to pay to break a lease. As a homeowner if the market is down, you could lose tens of thousands of dollars, as a renter it could cost you a few months rent.

THEY CAN'T FORECLOSE ON A RENTAL If tragedy strikes and you can no longer afford to live in a rental, you get evicted. If you can't make your home payments, they foreclose and you lose your home.

SOMEONE ELSE IS RESPONSIBLE FOR MAINTENANCE Sure, it can be a real pain in the tookus to deal with a rental company to get something fixed. In a house I rented, it took three weeks to get my refrigerator fixed. But, in a rental property, when the AC goes out, you are inconvenienced until it is fixed. As a homeowner, you are inconvenienced until it is fixed and you are out hundreds of dollars.

RENTING IS THROWING MONEY AWAY IS A MYTH Buying lotto tickets is throwing money away. Rent is not because you are getting a place to live in return. You have to live somewhere. It is not an "investment", but paying rent gives you shelter.

GETTING ONLY THE SPACE YOU NEED When you rent, more than likely, you will only rent the space you need. If you are living by yourself, you will only rent a one or two bedroom apartment. When people buy homes, oftentimes they buy much more than they need. People often end up with homes that have rooms in them they never go into to. This is a waste of space and money. By renting, you know you are only going to be in the space temporarily, therefore you only get what you need, thus saving you money. When people buy homes, they are not just thinking what they need now, but also what they might need in the future, and end up paying for space they don't need.

DEATH

Okay, I will admit it, the analogy had completely broken down. I have no way to talk about death in our house analogy. I can't say "demolition" because we are talking about preservation of the home after we are gone. Maybe we could call this section, "Building a Monument to You". Okay, maybe not.

Life Insurance: If You are Married

Once you decide that you need life insurance (which you do) the question is "How much insurance do I need?" The answer? A lot more than you think. Let's image that you die right now. I know it is grim thought, but it is one we must consider. First, let's figure out how much life insurance you would need to just to replace your income. If you make $30,000 a year, the answer is not $30,000. $30,000 will only provide for your absence for one year. Unless you expect the rest of your family to pick up the lost income, you will need more. If you want to provide your family with an income of $30,000 to replace your income, you will need enough money that the interest off the savings will produce $30,000 a year. If your family was to invest the money conservatively (which they should do because they need it to last) at 6% you would need a policy that paid out $500,000. To do the simple math with your income, take your income and divide by 0.06. All of this assumes that you believe that you are not going to receive a raise for the rest of your life, which probably isn't true.

Life Insurance: If You are Single

This is where I will depart from many of the financial books you will find in the bookstore. I am convinced everyone needs life insurance. I think for the sake of truthfulness, I need to make a disclosure. I am the son of an insurance salesman. My college degree, as well at many other things, was paid by the income generated from my father selling insurance. Even with that being said, I think the reasons are compelling enough that it will outweigh my possible bias. If you skipped the last section *Life Insurance: If You Are Married* because you are not married, go back and read it now. There is useful information about why life insurance is important in general. Go ahead, I'll wait.

The main reason you need to get some life insurance now (not as much as a married person needs), is because in the future it may become very difficult for you to get insurance. It is safe to say that you will never be younger or healthier than you are right now. Because of that fact, this is the cheapest life insurance will be for the rest of your life. You have no idea what ailment you could get later in life, and once you have these pre-existing conditions, it will be more expensive to get insurance. If you get insurance now, while you are healthy, as time passes your premium will go up because of your age, but it will not be affected if your health deteriorates in any way.

Leaving a Legacy to Your Children

In the sea of personal finance books, by far the best title of a book is DIE BROKE by Stephen Polland and Mark Levine. Besides being a great title, it is a very good book, though a little pessimistic. One of the main points of the book can be summed up in a quote from the introduction, "I tell my clients that the last check they write should be to the undertaker...and that it should bounce." They are not the only personal finance consultants to espouse this philosophy, but they explain the idea in greater detail than anyone you will find. Basically the argument goes like this...

First, inheritance is an antiquated idea which dates back to when the assets most people had was the land that they worked. The whole family worked the land as means for income. It made sense to pass that land from one generation to the next. Second, inheritance can become very destructive to a family before and after a generation dies. Children can get catty every time a parent makes a purchase, because it is part of their inheritance. Parents can lord inheritance over the next generation, forcing their kids to act in a particular way or risk losing what is coming to them. Then, when the parents die, the real fireworks can begin as kids fight over the estate like vultures. Third, when you pass money along in inheritance Uncle Sam comes in and takes his chunk. Believe me, there are very few in Washington who are fighting to cut the inheritance tax, because the dead don't vote or make campaign contributions (with the exception of Chicago).

Use your money now. First, it is a lot more fun to use the money when you are alive. If you decide to use it on and with your children and grandchildren now, you will get to see the joy in their lives. Second, a large gift is generally more useful early in life, as opposed to later. A ten thousand dollar gift to a couple in their twenties could be the down payment to their first house. Ten thousand dollars after your death to a couple in their fifties is a new sun room and hot tub. You can't take the money with you, and it is yours. Use it on yourself. Buy really cool stuff for your kids and grandkids. Give it away to charity. But die broke.

You still can't let this idea go that you want to leave something to your grandchildren. I have a simple idea. Leave them something small that will remind them at least once a year how wonderful you are and they should miss you. My grandfather owned a large chunk of stock in a small Illinois bank. On his death, he had a very detailed will. He gave each of the grandkids a percentage of his stock. The bank is well run, so every quarter we get a dividend check from the bank. It is not a large amount of money, usually around $100, but it is enough for a nice dinner with some good friends. Grandpa Gene is remembered and thanked a few times a year. A similar situation was set up by my mother's father as well. When we get the dividend check each year my mother always adds the note, "You grandfather would want you to spend this on something fun." In many ways, a small gift is better than a large gift. With a small gift, the giver is remembered, not the gift itself.

Wills

It is very simple. You must have a will. There are no i'fs, and's, or but's about it. It is a necessity. Unfortunately, most people do not have a will. If I were to hazard a guess why this is the case, I would guess it is because most people don't want to think about death, especially their own death. Get over it. You will die and if you want to take care of your family, you must have a will.

The reason you need a will is simple. When you die without a will, the state will decide where your money will go. First, the state will take care of all of your outstanding debt. Then the state distributes your assets according to state law and regulation, which vary greatly from state to state. Let's assume you are married, and have two children under the age of 16. When you die, I would assume you would want your assets to go to your spouse. If you don't have a will to express your wishes, then the laws of your locality will take effect. The state you live in might have a statute that says the assets of a deceased parent will go to the children in a trust to be given to them on their 18th birthday. So, instead of your spouse getting your assets to care for themselves and your children, the money is locked away until they are 18. Not what you, hoped I am sure. There is a very simple way to fix this: *Have a will.*

There are a number of things to consider when drafting a will. First, don't do it yourself. Get a professional to do it. If you open any phone book, you will find many lawyers who have this as a specialty. It shouldn't cost more than $300 to have a will written. This is really a bargain for all the hassle it will save your loved ones. The last thing they need is hassle while dealing with the loss of you.

Second, you will need to name an executor of the will. This is the person who will make sure your wishes are fulfilled. This needs to be someone who is honest, whom you trust. It is also helpful if they live near you. It might be difficult for them to travel to your home after death to do their job. In some cases, depending on your wishes, it could take a number of visits. Your executor should be someone who is your age or younger. No matter how much you trust your father, we can hope he is not the one who is going to bury you. You should ask the person before you list them as your executor. Having someone be your executor is kind of like giving someone a puppy as a present. What you are really doing is giving them work. It is also a good idea to name a contingent executor. Something could come up where your executor is not able to do the job. Having a back up is a good idea.

Third, keep your will up to date. As time passes, your life is going to change. You will add kids, homes, grandkids, and godchildren. When your kids are 10 and 12 it makes sense to have some of the money set aside to be put in a college fund for them, when they are 40 and 42, it doesn't. You should review your will once a year and make changes to your will with every major life change (eg births, marriages, deaths, divorces).

Finally, you need to make sure your executor knows where to find your will. You should send them a copy, keep a copy at home, and keep a copy in a safety deposit box. Also, you should keep an up-to-date list of assets with your will. This should include bank accounts, stocks and mutual funds, collectables, art, real estate, and everything else you own of value. Life for your executor could get complicated if 10 years later it is discovered you own stocks no one knew about.

Living Wills

In addition to having a will, it is a good idea to have a living will. A living will is nothing more than a legal document which describes your wishes in the case that you have become incapacitated. Most of the issues covered in a living will have to do with your care, such as, when to keep you on a respirator and for how long. Living wills have become very thorough. They cover every conceivable possibility. Many of them are pages and pages long that ask you questions about very specific situations allowing you describe your wishes for each. These are very touchy questions and you should spend time with your loved ones in making a living will. It is hard to look death square on like this, but again, get over it. You will die. If you plan for it now you, will make sure it is you who is making the choices and not the state.

COLLEGE

I won't insult you by trying to cram this into the analogy. This section is about paying for college.

Going to College.

Once again, it is important that I begin a section with full disclosure. I have a college degree, which I got at a wonderful private university. The only two contributions I made to fund my college education were that I paid for my books and my junior and senior years of college I was a resident assistand in freshmen resident halls. Being a resident assistant paid for my room and board which was about $7000 a year, about one third of my expenses. I qualified for some grants from the university which was about $6000 a year. The rest my parents paid. Even the student loans that were taken in my name, they are paying for. I am afraid to write this section because my parents might send me a bill. My parents were (and are) much too nice.

College is wonderful experience. I loved every moment of it. It was not the best years of my life, as some would contend. The best years of my life are the ones I am living now. Nonetheless, I loved it. It was a great opportunity to learn and grow. What is important to understand, is that it is just one way to learn and grow. It is not the only, or even the best way to learn and grow. College is not right for everyone. Even if college is the right thing to do, it might not be the right thing to do right now. Don't expect your kids to go to college because that is what "you are suppose to do" after graduating high school. Education is a wonderful thing. Getting an education holds a very high value in our culture. But it is important to look at the choice of going to college with the same sharp eye that you looked at how you want your life to look. It takes a lot of courage to say, "I am not going to get a high paying job, but be a social worker instead." To do this, you are having to cut across a large cultural tide. College is no different. Someone should only go to college because it the best choice for the life they want to craft.

The Value of College

We believe there is great value in education. It is part of the American fabric to equate education with a better life. When it comes time to consider college, it is not enough to ask if there is value in a college education. The real question is, *How much value does a college education have?* College is a place to gain skills. Most of the skills are gained in the classroom, but it can be argued that some skills are also gained from the rest of college life. But it must be clear, college is not some right of passage that makes our children adults. The education a student receives is a product. We are consumers. Colleges and universities are service providers. It is a marketplace. I hope talking about the great bastion of western civilization, education, as a commodity, isn't too offensive. Truth be told, that is what it is. Colleges and universities are businesses and you are spending lots of money with them. It is important to get the high-minded thought of education out of your head, at least for a few moments, and think about the true value of college. College is great, but it is not the only path. It is okay to follow your own path in the world. Ten years from now, college won't matter as much as what you are doing with your life at that moment. College is a tool. A college degree will improve your chance of getting some jobs, but it will not guarantee success. The average person will change careers more than four times in their life. Not just jobs or companies, most people will work in four different fields of work. As a matter of commerce, every day that passes, your college degree becomes less and less valuable. The only time your college degree will be on the top of your résumé is when you apply for that first job. After that, your experience will be listed first. College is not bad, but understand it for what it is. There are successful people who never went to college or dropped out and many unsuccessful people who graduated from Ivy League schools.

Also, when considering the value of college, it is important to challenge the notion that an 18 year old has any idea what she wants to do with his life. I work with high school students for a living. Oftentimes I work with leadership teams of high school students. I see the best of the best. Many of them, at eighteen, have no idea what they want to do with their lives. This is completely reasonable. There are days at 30 in which I wake up wondering if I know what I want to do with my life. I think back to my college experience and the maturity I possessed at the time. I think back to the choices I made. Yikes. It is embarrassing. I took classes, not because of what I would be learning, but because it was an easy A. $1200 was spent on an easy A. I promise you, that if I went back to school now, I would do it in a completely different way. There would be very little wasted time or effort. I would be there with a very clear goal of what I wanted to get out of my education. If the value of college is the education that will improve your child's prospect of success, then sending your child to an expensive private four year college may not be the best value.

So if your child goes off to college, God bless them, but they should only go to the college you can afford. I am sorry if I have been a bit of a buzzkill. I am just afraid that our sense of the value of college has been clouded. Think this through for a minute. If your child walked in, asked you to buy him a brand new sports car, you wouldn't do it. It is way too much. All he really needs is transportation. A more reasonably priced car makes much more sense. For some reason, we feel if our child wants to go to a particular university, it is our responsibility to pay for it. That is ridiculous.

Getting Value for Your Education Spending

When considering your education options it is important to broaden your perspective.

STATE SCHOOLS Instead of going to a small private school, which they ask for your first born to attend, you can go to a cheaper state school. There are many wonderful state schools which provide a great education many times at one third the cost of a comparable private school.

START AT COMMUNITY COLLEGE You can also go to a local community college for two years to get all the basics taken care of, then head off to another more expensive school. When it comes to getting the basics, there is very little difference between the curriculums of a Calculus class from one school to the next. Why would you pay $2000 for a Calculus at a private school, when you can get basically the same class for one fifth that at a community college? Some might argue the private school education is better. I don't agree. Even if that argument is granted, I doubt you could be persuaded to believe it is five times better.

PART TIME It is not written in stone somewhere that everyone needs to be a full time college student. It could be more reasonable for your child to go to school part time. There are a number of advantages to going to school part time. First, your child will be making money while she is going to school. It is not a situation of just money going out the door. Second, as a full time student, you live in a bubble. Your whole life is campus life. In a lot of ways, it is very easy to lose touch with reality. If someone is also working a job while in college, they will get a much better feel of what *the real world* is like. It might encourage your child to be a better student. Also, by having to work a job, your child might get the sense of what type of work they don't want to do. There is one final possible advantage to being a part time student. There are lots of companies that pay for tuition of their employees. Companies see investing in the education of their employees as an investment in the future of the company itself. It is possible to be taking home a paycheck, go to school, and have someone pay for the schooling. There is no crime in being a part time student and working.

Student Loans

If it requires you to get loans to go a school, you cannot afford it. Under no circumstance, should you take college loans for yourself or your children. It is not worth it. Why would you want to send someone off into the world with $10,000 (or more) in debt? As reported by Brian Knestout of KIPLINGER'S PERSONAL FINANCE, the average graduate from the 100 best private colleges graduated with an average debt of $16,524* and $14,794** for 100 best public colleges and universities. If you want your children to do what they love in life, why would you send them out into the world already in the hole?

When I say, "Don't take student loans," I mean every student loan. It might be enticing to take a federally subsidized loan. A federally subsidized loan is a loan in which the federal government pays the interest on the loan while the student is still in school. Once you are no longer the loan starts gathering interest. It can feel like free money. It's not. This is still a loan. Do not do it. It is not worth it. Think of all the work it will be to get out of debt for your child. When you did your budgeting, remember all the cuts you had to make out of your life to get rid of your debt? Don't start them out on the wrong foot.

How Not To Pay For College

Okay, so you are a big softy. You want you children to go to the college they want (which isn't a bad thing). I know I would want the same if I had kids (which would probably mean I would need to get a date first, but that is another story). But only do this, if this is something you want. Educating your children so they can be self-sufficient members of society is your job as a parent, sending them to a college that costs thirty thousand dollars a year is not.

If you are going to do some saving for your child's college education you need to start right now. If it is your child's junior year of high school, it is too late. Looking at the numbers above, a college degree from a private school could cost as much as a house or two. The more time you are saving money, the better. If you think someday you are going to have kids and you would like to help them with there college expenses, it is a good idea to start right now.

---

* http://moneycentral.msn.com/content/CollegeandFamily/Cutcollegecosts/P71026.asp
**http://www.kiplinger.com/tools/colleges/pubcollege.php?sortby=INRANK03&orderby=flip&states%5B%5D=ALL&myschool%5B%5D=none&outputby=table

Right now you might be panicking, thinking it is too late. If this is you, there three things you need to do. First, take a deep breath. It is going to be okay. Second, re-read the last section. There are lots of other options besides a really expensive school. Third, you will promise yourself, right now, that you will not make any of the following mistakes:

HOME EQUITY LOAN You can't turn on the television without seeing some ad for a great new home equity loan. The argument is something like, "These are the lowest rates in years. Refinance now. Use the money for home improvements, a vacation, or to pay for you kid's college tuition." At first glance, it makes sense. The way a home equity loan works, is a bank is willing to loan you the value of your home and you put up your home as equity. Equity means nothing more in this context than if you don't pay back the loan, they take your house. After you receive a loan for the value of your house, you then take part of that money to pay off the original home loan you have. Since you have been making payments on your home for years, the remaining amount on the original loan should be less than the value of your house. Since the new loan is the value of your home, after you pay off the old loan you now have money left over to use as you would like. You are thinking to yourself, "This is great. We can keep making the same payment (or maybe a payment which is a little less), and have money to pay for college." There is one fact you are not taking into account here. You payments may be the same, but the number of years that you will have to make those payments has just increased. For example, you bought your home when you were about thirty and you received a 30 year loan to pay for the house. For those thirty years you plan to make all your payments in a timely fashion. When you are sixty years old, the home is paid off. As part of your retirement planning you knew that when you retire at 65 the home was going to be paid for, so you knew you were going to need to save a little less, because you would have no housing expense. Instead, at 45, you decide to take out a home equity loan to pay for college for one of your children. It, as well, is a 30 year loan. Instead of having your home paid off at 60, it will not happen until 75 (because the new loan is 30 years starting when you are age 45). If you still retire at 65, that will leave you with house payment for 10 years while you are retired. This will not work.

BORROW FROM YOUR OWN RETIREMENT This is a bad idea for two reasons. First, you are sabotaging your own retirement. I don't want to come off as callous and mean, but your retirement is important. It is not worth it for you to jeopardize your future for your children to get a college degree (which they won't be using in ten years). Second, it just doesn't make any business sense. When you put your money into an IRA for your retirement, the income you receive is tax deferred.

Meaning you don't have to pay any tax on the income, until you take the money out. Not only will the money you take out of your IRA be taxed, the moment it is used to pay for your child's college, there is an added penalty. Since you are getting a tax break for saving money in a IRA, the IRS wants to make sure that you are really using the money for retirement. You are not just saving money in a tax free fashion to buy a new car. So, if you remove money from your retirement fund before retirement age, besides the taxing that happens, there is also a 10% penalty. So it's a double whammy and not a good business move.

PRE PAID TUITION PLANS There is a new plan which many colleges are offering. What colleges are offering is the opportunity for you to pay for college now, at today's costs. When your child is college-age, she then gets to attends school, with the tuition paid for. The selling point is, "You know tuition is going up six or seven percent a year. Pay at today's prices and save." Seems like a reasonable proposition, but there are more than a few problems. What if your child doesn't want to go to that school? You will get a refund, but with little or no return on the investment. This is the equivalent of saving for college by putting the money in a mayonnaise jar in the basement, and pulling it out when it is time for your child to head off to college. Would you have trusted your parents to pick your college when you were six years old? Well, you might think, "My child should be happy that I am paying for his schooling at all. If I am going to pay, this is where he should go." You are right, your child should be very happy you are paying for his schooling, but what happens if you have chosen a school that doesn't have your child's chosen field of study. Your son longs to be a dentist, but the school you have done the pre-pay plan with, doesn't have dentistry as a major. Second problem. What if your child doesn't get into the school? Just because you have done a pre-pay plan, doesn't mean she is guaranteed a spot at the school. I am sure your daughter is the brightest kid in her class (everyone's child is), but there is a real possibility she might not get in. Yes, you get your money back, but not with a return on the investment. Another possible problem is the fact you could incur a tax liability. You pre pay $10,000. When your child gets to college the tuition is $70,000. The IRS will see your invested $10,000 and received a return of $60,000. You must pay taxes on that $60,000. Fourth, these programs only pay for tuition. They do not pay for room and board, which can be as much as one third of the total college expense. Finally, these programs many not be around by the time your child is college age. Some schools are already canceling them, others are changing the terms to have them only cover a percentage of total tuition.

How To Save for Your Child's College Expenses

Relax. There is hope. I promise. There is actually a very good way to save for your children's college education. It is called a 529 Plan. 529 plans were created by the federal government specifically for educational savings. 529 plans can only be administrated by the states. Every state offers at least one. In almost every case the states have contracted the work out to someone in the private sector. 529 plans are just like any other mutual fund you will find on the market. Much like IRA, the money invested in a 529 is tax free. Until 2010, when you take the money out of the fund to pay for college expenses (included room and board) it is also federal tax free (state tax varies from state to state). At this point, after 2010, you will have to pay taxes on only the dividend (the revenue generated). It is possible that Congress will extend this date.

There are no state residency requirements for investing in a state's plan. Which means you can enroll in any plan you would like. You can redirect which person you would like to use the savings plan for. This means that you can create one account for all your children to use if you would like. If you do decide to have one account for each child, and one child decides not to go to college or doesn't use all the money, then it can be very easily used for another child. You can open the account, even if you don't have children, knowing someday you might. Finally, anyone can make a contribution to the account.

This sounds great, where is the catch? There are only two things to consider. First, if you make a withdrawal from the account for non-qualified distributions (meaning non-education related withdrawals) you will have to pay the income tax plus a 10% penalty. Second, there are only a limited number of funds in which you can invest in. As mentioned above, only states are allowed to run these programs. When it comes to creating an IRA for your retirement, you can choose any investment option you want. Here, your choices are limited. This mean one thing, you will have to do your home work. Just like any other investment, you will need to know::

- the history of the rate of return
- what fees you are being charged
- how diversified is the portfolio
- everything else you would look into when making any investment

As time passes, if the fund you have invested in starts doing poorly, you can move the funds to another 529.

Finally, two notes of caution. First, one of the great advantages of 529 plans is the fact that the money is controlled by the person who has started the account, not who the account is for. This is far superior to save for a child in the child's name. There are some minor tax implications to that, but more significantly, the biggest reason is when the child turns 18 year old. They will control the money. Imagine this, you have scrimped and saved so that your son can go to college, he turns 18, takes the money and buys a car. The money is in his name. He is now an adult. It is his money.

The second note of caution revolves around others making contributions to 529 plans. It is a wonderful thing when someone else takes an interest in your child's education, like your parents. But be careful. If you read the fine print above, the person who starts the account is the one who determines where the money will go. That means grandma might add money to the account for one child, but in the end the person who started the account has say so of where the money goes, regardless of grandma's wishes. I am not saying you are going to set up a 529 to fleece your relatives, but people get funny around money. They don't act rationally, especially when you add family ties. Do what you need to do, but just keep all this in mind.

HOW TO TITHE

I know, at this point, you head is spinning at the amount of money you now realize you need to put away for retirement. The last thing you want to do is think of tithing, but it is something we are all called to do. Even as we struggle to make ends meet, simply by the fact that you could afford to buy this book, and take the time to read, it means that by "world standards" you are better off than most. (If you have a computer in your home you, are better off than 97 percent of the population of the planet Earth).

When it comes to answering these questions, I have found it helpful to create a portfolio of my tithing. If you are not familiar with the word "portfolio", it is very simple. A portfolio is nothing more than a collection. An artist has a portfolio of all her work. She uses this as a way of showing others the scope of her work. In terms of investing, "portfolio" refers to all of your investments. A portfolio can be very simple, (a few mutual funds and a college fund) or it can very complicated (stocks, bonds, foreign currency, and expensive wine). When I look at the way I am tithing, I create a portfolio as well. By this, I mean I create a collection of ways that I give that reflects a number of different criteria. I have found that if I am intentional about helping in a number of different ways, it has helped me be a well-rounded person, with a much clearer view of what is going on in the world and how I fit into it. There are three basic questions that I ask myself when I am considering tithing: *What do I have to give? Where should I give?* and *How much should I give?* Let's examine all three.

WHAT DO I HAVE TO GIVE? The assets you have to offer are your time, talents and treasure. So often when we think of tithing, we do only in terms of the money we have to offer. I feel that many times giving money (though important) is a bit of a cop out. Just write a check to some far off charity helping those people who really need it. We've helped and our conscience feels better. But are we truly aware of who is being helped and what their plight is? By investing your time or talent in an organization or cause, you will become much more intimately aware of who you are helping and why they need help. Oftentimes, the gift of the time and talent is more helpful than a simple check.

WHERE SHOULD I GIVE? There are at least three types of considerations to take into account: *Where to support? What type of organization to support?* and *What type of work to support?* First, *Where to support?* Often, it is easiest to respond to the needs in your local community because those are the problems you see and are the problems that affect you directly. Or you will choose a cause that is close to you personally. You have a close friend or relative who has MS so you put your time and efforts into that cause. Those are wonderful reasons for supporting organization and causes, but I would challenge you to also look larger. As it was said recently, "Compassion does not stop at the Rio Grande". We are part of a big world that has many problems. Although we can't see these problems in our daily life, those who suffer from them are part of the Body of Christ who need our support. Don't just look locally. Just because you don't have contact doesn't mean they don't need your help. I think it is important to strike a balance between helping locally and globally. The second consideration is, *What types of organizations to support?* Oftentimes, when people are thinking about tithing, they think since the motivation to help is spiritually based that organization and cause that one is to support needs to also be spiritually-based. I don't think this is necessary true. There are many causes and organizations that often are done more effectively in a secular context. It is important to consider these organizations as well. The final consideration: *What type of work to support?* There are basically two types of work that an organization can do: direct service and social justice. In most cases an organization's thrust will be one or the other, but an organization may participate in both. The difference between the two types of work is very simple. Direct service is simply what the name implies. When an organization is doing direct service, they are meeting the needs of their constituency directly. They are feeding people. They are providing healthcare. They are teaching people to read. Basically, they are meeting immediate needs now. Social justice is work that addresses the system which perpetuates the situation. Social justice works to bring down the cost of health care to make it more affordable. It educates about, and advocates for, a particular cause, so others are more aware of it. It does research to create a vaccine to prevent a particular disease. It becomes very easy to see how these two types of service work in concert with each other. If we only meet the immediate needs we might stop short term suffering. But the problem would only continue in the future. If only social justice work was done, then we might eradicate problems, but would do nothing for those who are suffering now.

How much to give? Is it 10% of what you make before and after taxes? If I am giving 10 hours a month in service, does that mean I should give less money? This is the area in which I can provide the least amount of guidance. What I can do is recommend an exercise. Find a local organization in which you believe in their mission. Go to the organization and see how they work. Meet the people who run to organization. Meet the people that the organization services. Basically, come face-to-face with the Body of Christ that is being served and is at work. Get to know those who are working for the cause. Get to know personally the plight of those who are being served. When you bump into the Body of Christ that is present in all parts of the organization, you will know what you can give. Your giving will not be coming out of some rule or edict, but out of your personal relationship with the Body of Christ.

After asking these questions, try creating a portfolio of your tithing. I will not offer hard and fast rules. You need to construct a plan that fits your life and your desires. Make some rules you can work by. Maybe you want to give 7% of your post-tax income, 8 hours a month, and use your web development skills. Your time and talent will be given to a local cause and you will do a 60/40 split on your financial contribution to a local/global organization. You decide to give your local energies to agencies that specialize in direct service and your global energies will be to an organization that works mostly in the social justice arena. There are an infinite number of combinations, and there is no right way to do it. But build a system that fits your life. If you consider many of these criteria not only will you be feeding the Body of Christ, but you will force yourself to be more aware of the plight of the Body of Christ, how much you are connected to that, and how you can grow in relation to it.

Other Ways to Help

One thing that I did not mention that you can offer, is your prayers. When you decide to "adopt" a cause or organization, do it also spiritually. Not only pray for the organization and those they serve, but pray specifically for those who are doing the service. Fulltime service work is very rewarding, but also very challenging. Many times, those who have chosen that line of work have made many sacrifices of themselves and their families. They could use our prayers.

Know Who You Are Working With

A final caution that I would offer, is to make sure the organization that you are supporting is truly doing the work that they say they are doing. I am not asking you to be suspicious of someone's motives (and I am not naive enough to believe that there are no cons out there), but I think it is just as important to look at how an organization is using its contributions for the cause it has chosen. If an organization is spending over half of it's resources on fundraising, is that the best way they can spend their money? It is important that we hold the organization we contribute to a high level of stewardship. For example, you have been called by organization X to come down and help them out on a Saturday afternoon and you agree. The weekend comes. You get up early to get all your Saturday errands in before showing up. Once you get there, no one is there to meet you. After waiting thirty minutes someone finally shows up, but they "aren't the one in charge of volunteers" and "don't know what they have planned for you that day." Thirty minutes latter the volunteer coordinator finally shows up. It takes them thirty minutes to get settled in for the day, and finally turn to you to give you your task, which lasts a total of thirty minutes. "I guess I thought we had more work for you. Lucky for you, you are done." You think, "Yeah, lucky for me, I rearranged my Saturday so I could give 2 hours, not including travel time, to do thirty minutes of work." The volunteer coordinator asks you on your way out the door, "Can we call you again sometime?" Not wanting to be rude you say, "Sure," knowing full well the next time they call, you will be "busy." Who could blame you? You are not a horrible person. You want to help, but your time is valuable and they just wasted it.

The resources you have to give, are limited. Expect organizations to respect your money, as much as you would expect them to respect your time. Before you make a contribution to an organization, make sure you understand not only the mission of the organization, but how exactly they meet those needs and how they use their money. It is okay to ask those questions. Charitable organizations get those questions all the time. They should be more than willing to answer those questions. And if they are not, you might want to seriously reconsider donating to them.

Giving With Joy

Cheryl was very happy that we were in an Anglophone country (one that speaks a version of English). At the time, she was a Peace Corp volunteer in Benin, Africa. Some of the Benewah spoke French (which Cheryl spoke) and everyone spoke Phon (the language of the old Donhomi kingdom). Being in Ghana, everyone spoke a language she understood (it was first time in my trip that I was able to speak to non-Americans without being translated). The most exciting prospect of Sunday, was the fact Cheryl was going to get to go to church in English.

At the taxi stand near our hotel, we caught a cab. The driver assured us he knew where the church was. Really, he knew the area of town we were looking for, but the church itself was a little elusive. After driving in circles for ten minutes, we found it. The gathering had begun, so we slipped into the last row.

The service itself was amazing. Three choirs sung at different points during the celebrations. The congregation was celebrating the birthday of Mary and a group of seven year old girls came out and sang "Happy Birthday" to Mary. In addition to the verse we all know to Happy Birthday, they also sang a bunch of verses about her life as a faithful servant. Sometimes, the whole group sang and other times, just a few. There were even a few solos. There was such a sense of community and celebration.

It came time for the collection. Instead of passing a basket around, a basket was placed in the front and everyone brought forward their gift. At this point I had been to a number of services in other parts of Africa. Most religious services mirror daily life in Africa in this regard. There are no lines...ever. If you are checking out of a store, you just push to the register. If you are getting on a plane, you just push to the door. At church, when it comes time to give your donation, you just walk up to the basket, when you are ready. Apparently, that was not the case here. Instead, we were to file from the back row to the front, in a ordered fashion.

We were in the last row because of our late arrival. The woman who was the usher on our side, figured out immediately that we were guests (being that we were the only two whites in the congregation of over 1,500). She leaned in with a face that was as wide as it was tall, skin dark as night, and a white smile that was as wide as her face. She said, "This is the time we bring our gifts forward." She paused and moved to let me out of pew. As I was about to hesitantly get up she leaned back in and, eyes glowing with joy, she said, "And you can dance if you want."

By this point the people in other sections of the church were starting to file forward bringing their gifts, and they were dancing. So, for the first time I can ever remember, I got up and danced without embarrassment and brought my gift forward with the true joy of giving.

Tithing is an important part of the human experience. Even though tithing isn't about us, we do get a lot out of it. Don't give because you have too. Open yourself up to those you are blessed to serve and those you serve along side with. It is in these moments that we discover our humanity, in these experience we come to understand more fully, how we are connected to one another. Don't just give your time, talent, and treasure. Give your joy. It will be returned ten-fold.

PART V

More Tools

Wasting Time

Over and over again, throughout this book, I have taken a number of pot shots at television. Some have been veiled; others have been haymakers. I have nothing against television. My mother takes great joy in making fun of the fact that whenever I talk about TV shows I really like, I will parrot the phase, "smart, funny, and so well written" (see THE SIMPSONS, M*A*S*H, SPORTS NIGHT, HOMICIDE). There is some good, even great, television out there. There is wonderful storytelling about the human condition. There is amazingly brilliant comedy. You might have to work hard to find it, but it is there. The problem I found in my own life with television, was the amount of time I was spending with really bad television. I would flip for hours, never really landing on something, but somehow losing four hours of my life.

One of the great battles of living a life with passion is using the time you have. When it comes to crafting our lives, we only have three things at our disposal: our talent, our time, and our treasure. We have to manage all three of them well. Because of my ADHD, it is so easy for me to lose whole days of my life. I will simply flitter from one thing to the next, never getting anything done. That is the primary reason that I am so fanatical about my daily goal list. By looking at my goal list three times a day, I keep re-reminding myself what I want my life to look like. It is not enough to simply look at the list of tasks I need to get done. I need to keep showing myself why those tasks are important.

I also don't want you to misconstrue my sentiment here to think I want you to become a goal driven machine. I am not expecting you to be working off your task list from the moment you get up till the moment you go to bed. What I am suggesting is that you choose how you want to invest your time. On my visit to the orphanage/school Santa Maria del Mexicano, I was amazed by their schedule. During the school year, every minute of a student's day was spoken for. From 6:30 AM when they got up, until 8:00 PM when they went to bed. Their day was filled with school, prayer, working in the fields, and studying. But it was also filled with play. Once during the school day, and for a big chunk of time in the evening, they we able to play–just to be the kids they are. They are either from bad family situations or no family at all. Many of them are academically behind the average student of their age. The school understands the kids need to work hard to gain stability in their lives and to get caught up. The kids also need discipline to function in society. Regardless of their hard pasts and the strides they needed to make, they are still kids, and need to be kids. They need to play. Not only are they given time to play; they are allowed to be kids all day. During the time the kids had to work in the afternoon, either in the fields or around the school, they were still allowed to be kids. They were certainly expected to do their jobs, but they didn't have an armed warden lording it over them, acting as the fun police. They got their work done and were still able to laugh with eachother while doing it.

Hopefully, working through this book you have allowed youself to dream of what your life could really look like. Hopefully, it is a big enough dream that it is going to take a fair bit of work to get there (meaning that your life will be that much richer). It is important that you work hard to reach the life you want, but it is important you enjoy the journey. I hope you become serious about taking control of your life, but not too serious. Like the kids of Santa Maria Del Mexicano, I hope you take time for recess. I hope you take time to eat good food with friends. I hope you take time to watch movies. I hope you take time to play on the swing set. Just make sure you are choosing to do what you most want to do. Spending three hours with good friends, sharing life, is not wasting time. At the same time very few things can kill the possibility of dreams coming true like wasting time. You should now have a plan (even if it is a vague plan) of what your life can look like. Each day, you only have so much time. After the minutes pass, you can't get them back. The trick is striking the balance.

Getting Organized

A topic that goes hand in hand with not wasting time, is getting organized. It is simply not enough to eliminate the time wasters of your life (though that is a great start). I have found in my own life that by getting organized, I make better use of my time. This is not a revolutionary thought. I know you have thought to yourself, "If I could just get myself a little more organized, I would be way ahead of the game." There are a few things you can do to make it easier to get yourself organized.

First, find a system that works for you. There is no end all, be all, best way to do this. Each of us has a different learning style. A system that works for me might make your day more hectic. The topic of organization is way too big to get into the how to's here. I would highly recommend Brian Tracy's book EAT THAT FROG. In a hundred quick-reading pages, he covers 21 different ways to get yourself organized. I re-read the book twice a year. In my own life I have used a number of the ideas from the book and crafted a system that works for me.

Second, you are going to need to consciously work at the system you create before it becomes habit. Not only is it going to require some trial and error to get a system that works for you, but you are also going to be fighting all your old bad habits. Most of the organizational systems I have created for my own life have lasted about a week. It is not that the system wasn't right for me. Instead, after a week, I lost my commitment to it. In the beginning, it might feel like things are taking you more time. That is because you are doing things in a new way, not because it is a bad system. The trick is to fight with your system until it becomes habit for you.

Third, you need to stop lying to yourself. You can no longer look at the clutter on your desk and say, "It may look like a mess, but I know where everything is." And yes, I know, you have had the experience of cleaning up your office and then when you look for something, you can't find it. We have all made the comment, "I knew exactly where that was before I cleaned my office." More than likely, it's because you did nothing more than clean off the surfaces of your office. You got everything out of site. You didn't organize it. The chaos needs to stop right now. We have all used the excuse, "I do my best work at the last minute." Wrong! It might feel more exciting to be working on a deadline, but there is no way you work better at the last minute. I can't believe that working in a sleep-deprived state, and only doing something once without review, helps you create better work. If you did projects in a timely fashion you would get the opportunity to refine your work again and again. There is no way you can convince me that a rushed job at the last minute is better. Get rid of all the excuses in your life. Get more organized. If the only two benefits you received from getting yourself organized were higher quality work, and more free time, that would be more than enough.

Business Plan

When Brad and I started our ministry, the first thing we did was write a business plan. We took six weeks to look at the skills we had and the marketplace where we could take those skills. The document we created was beautiful. It was twenty three pages long. Oooooooh! Very impressive, I know. (Please note the author's sarcasm.) I can very vividly recall the end of this process. We read over the whole document together. Brad looked up and said, "This is the most organized I have ever been!" He paused and asked rhetorically (because he knew the answer), "We've only just started, right?"

Anyone who has ever written a business plan, will tell you the goal of writing a business plan is not the plan itself, but the process that you go through. Writing a business plan forces you to figure out the mission of the business, how you are going to implement that vision; the obstacles you are going to face, what the financial structure of the organization is going to be; and the resources you are going to need to use. I hope this sounds familiar. If you have been doing all of the exercises of this book, you have been writing the plan for your life. The goals you have created for your life reflect how the mission of your life is executed. You have done budgeting and financial planning for the future. You have named the obstacles you think you are going to face and planned how to get around them. You have figured out the resources you are going to use to help you reach your goals. You have named ways you are going to know you are successful.

Just like the business planning process, the paperwork you have created is not the most important product (though you are going to keep using the goals list and budget tools). What is most important, is the process that you have gone through. In the process, you have had the chance to flesh out your vision and to see how it fits into the world. By processing through the possibilities, you have seen the possible obstacles and pitfalls. You are ready for them. But just like a business plan, the planning means little if you don't start.

Coach or Support Group.

One of the most difficult aspects of money, is the taboo we have surrounded the topic. As a society, we have become more and more permissive in the topics it is okay to talk about. Politics, religion, and even sex are common-place conversation topics, but not money. We will talk with friends about hopes and dreams, medical advice, and how to raise children, but not money. It is not something that is brought up in polite conversations and, in many cases, it is not even a topic that is appropriate for family to talk about. Think how insulting it would be to ask someone how much money they make in a year? This taboo stems from the fact that many of us equate our self-worth to the money we have or make. Money is nothing more than a tool. A very important tool, but a tool nonetheless.

I think it is important to find a support system to talk about all the issues we are discussing here. You need to find a way to talk about hopes, dreams, and how money is a part of that plan. There are two ways of doing this. First, get a coach. This coach is like every other coach. The coach's job is to guide and encourage. They have a clip board and whistle. They know what the game plan is. Sometimes they provide a kind word. Other times, they kick your butt when you need it. Most importantly, they meet with you regularly. When I was first starting to understand my learning disabilities, at age 19, I had a coach whom I talked to everyday. My coach knew exactly what my goals were for the day. At the end of each day, we talked on the phone and I gave a report of my day. Many times during the day I would be faced with a decision, and the only thing that motivated me to make the right choice, was the fact that at the end of the day, I was going have to report to my coach. As time passed, the choices became easier and easier as they became habit.

Another option to finding a support, is to start a group. Instead of having one person provide support for you, you can create a community in which you support each other. Find a group of people who are willing to meet regularly to talk about your dreams. Hold each other accountable. Share your successes. Encourage each other. Get together every month or two, buy some nice wine, have a big meal, pray together, and talk about your lives. And most importantly, talk about money. Find people you trust so that you can all be honest.

There are lots of fruits from talking about issues in our lives. Often, we receive advice and help from those with more experience than us, but I think there is something much more important at work here. Oftentimes in conversation, the two greatest fruits are that we hear, out loud, our struggles, and see they are not as big as we thought, and that we have someone who is sitting across from us who says nothing more than, "Yeah, I know." It is a powerful experience to know that we are not alone in what we are facing. It is amazing how much power our anxieties lose when they get out of our heads and into the light.

Celebrate Your Successes Big and Small

As you move down this path, you are going to be faced with lots of choices. Some of the choices are going to move you closer to the life you want, while others are not. Whenever you make a choice that does not move you closer to your dream, don't beat yourself up. Don't lament what might have been. Take time to look at the choices you made. Figure out what you would do differently, learn, and move on. You are going to face enough obstacles along the way. The last thing you want to do is create more by beating yourself up over bad choices and missed opportunity.

In the same vein, it is also important to acknowledge all of your successes. I know that when I do a good job and am recognized by others, not only do I feel better but I'm more motivated to move forward. Success breeds success. When you move forward, it is important celebrate. Now the celebration should be in proportion to the accomplishment. Just because you got up early and ran this morning, doesn't mean you should have all the neighbors over for a party, but something small would be appropriate. Maybe you just do a little happy dance. How you dance is not important. The fact that you are dancing is important. Never compare your accomplishment to other people. The standard that you are living up to is you. It may be nothing for your spouse to go a day without eating any candy. For you, it might take every ounce of energy. If you did a good job today, celebrate!

You Need to Recommit

The water was not potable (meaning it wasn't drinkable) at our housing in Mexico City. I travel more internationally than the average person. I am still shocked at the things I take for granted, such as easily available (seemingly unlimited) drinkable water. We were required to use bottled water for just about everything, including brushing our teeth. Every time I would brush my teeth, I would half fill a small Styrofoam cup with bottled water and head to the bathroom. One small pour to wet the toothpaste. One small pour to rinse my brush. One drink to slosh around my mouth. This would leave me enough left over to take a drink. I brushed my teeth with 4 oz. of water.

After doing this three or four times, it struck me how much water I wasted when I brushed my teeth at home. Each time I need more water, I just let the water run. I am not a complete heathen; I don't let the faucet run the whole time. I am turning it on and off for each step, but still so much is going by unused. So right then and there, standing in my pajamas in Mexico City, I decided to turn over a new leaf. From that moment on, I was no longer going to waste water when I brushed my teeth. Trumpets blared! Choirs of angels began to sing praises! Okay. Bit of an overstatement, but great things begin with small steps. I was taking one small (more than likely very small) step to help the environment.

And then...it happened. Two days later, we found ourselves in housing that had purified water, and just like that, I had forgotten my commitment. I was right back to my old ways. Old habits. Taking action without thinking of the outcome. This went on for a couple of days, my water-wasting ways. A few days passed. On day three, it dawned on me. Once again I was wasting water. I stopped and thought "how easy I forget." So I recommitted to the cause. For the rest of my time in Mexico, I was faithful to my pledge.

And then I came home. It was only as I was writing about the trip for some friends, that I realized that once again I had forgotten my pledge. Once again I had reverted to my old ways of waste. Once again, reconsidered of who I want to be, I commit again to not waste.

I'm sure you can relate. Right now, I hope you are brimming with excitement. For the first time in a long time, you feel like you are gaining control of your life. You can almost taste what life is going to be. That feeling is going to pass. Sorry. It is just the truth. Right now is like the time before you have asked someone out on a first date and the date itself. Everything is perfect. You find yourself at work staring out the window, day dreaming of the date to come and the beautiful child you are going to have. Right now is the easiest it is going to be. Which means it is only going to get harder from here. The obstacles you are expecting are going to be harder than you think. There are the obstacles you don't expect lurking out there as well. You are going to fall back into your bad habits after making progress. You are going to backslide. There are even going to be times when you feel further from your destination than you are now. I know, because it happens to me too.

There is nothing you can do to stop this from happening. The obstacles are going to come. The doubt is going to creep back in. Really, if it was easy, you would have fixed things a long time ago. Since you can't stop temporary failure, there are few things you can do to combat loss of hope.

First, you need to name when doubt is creeping in. When you start to feel the presence of doubt, turn to it and say, "I see you doubt. Right now you are trying to sabotage what I am tryingto do. You are the one who is telling me I am not good enough, that I am not talented enough, that I am not strong enough to do this. You are wrong! Not only can I do this, I am going to do it." I am not kidding. I really want you to say something like that. If you feel silly saying that out loud, say it in your head. It will have more power if you say it out loud. If you have to, go lock yourself in a closet so no one will see or hear you. When you are lying in bed before you fall asleep at night, these negative thoughts are going to creep in. You must fight them off!

Second, there are times in which you are going to fail at one of the steps along the way. Failure is a good thing. Really! It provides an opportunity for learning.

Many modern inventors are not trying to find faster ways to produce their products, but instead they are trying to find faster ways to fail. Failure can show you not only what doesn't work, but what does work. David Bayles and Ted Orland point to this phenomenon in their book, ART AND FEAR. They explain that there was a college pottery class which was broken into two groups. One group was going to be graded on quality. They would only have to turn one pot in at the end of the semester. That one pot would be their full grade. The other group was going to be graded on quantity. The last day of the semester they were to bring in all the work they had done, so it could be weighed. Fifty pounds would get an 'A', forty a 'B' and so on. At the end of the semester, the group that had produced the best work was the group that was graded on weight. Because they needed to make so many pots, they were given lots of opportunities to make mistakes, and learn from their mistakes. The group graded on quality spent lots of time figuring out what quality was, but not making it work. They thought big thoughts, but didn't get better.

You are going to make mistakes. After you have failed, take a step back and review what has happened. Look at every step you just took. What assumptions did you have that were wrong? If you could do it over again, what choices would you make differently? What choices would you make again? What new piece of information did you learn? What piece of information did you confirm you were right about? Learn. Then move on. Really, move on. It is okay to regret the choices you have made. This provides an opportunity for learning. Lament, on the other hand, becomes debilitating. If you stay with the failure and regret the poor choices you made and the opportunities you missed, you will not be able to deal with what you need to do next. Maybe this new experience will let you know that your whole plan is wrong. That's okay. It is better you know that now than later. With your newfound knowledge, decide what you need to do next.

Third, what you are working on right now, is just a detail. In my past life, I was a computer programmer. Every week, my team would gather for a status meeting. To start, everyone in the group would update the rest of the group on the week's progress. I was in charge of a large chunk of code. Over the course of the week, we had come across a problem that we could not solve. It was a technical hurdle we could not get over. Basically, in our mind this was the end of the project. There was no way around this problem. We were done. It shook the whole foundation to the ground. My manager turned to me and said, "That's just a detail." I tried to explain. Maybe he didn't hear clearly. We were done. Finished. Bereft of life. Rung down the curtain and joined the choir invisible. WE WERE TOAST! My manager said, "I understand how you feel. It is just a detail." He then moved on with the rest of the meeting. I was stunned, and a little punch drunk, and headed back to my computer. Three of us worked around the clock for the next 48 hours (literally) and solved the problem. My manager was right. It was just a detail. In the big picture of what we were trying to accomplish, it wasn't that big of a deal. In the moment, it was, and deserved the intense attention it received from the three of us.

Keep reminding yourself what the end goal is. Oftentimes, it is very easy for us to get caught up in the step we are taking right now. We lose track of the big picture. When you are faced with failure or doubt or both, pull out your goal sheet again. Look at what the big picture is going to be like. Is your dream worth fighting through the current struggle? Duh? Yes it is! Take a deep breath. Go for a long walk. Get a good night's sleep. Forget about what you are trying to achieve for a few days. Lick your wounds. Don't feel sorry for yourself, but gain a little perspective.

Your Original Vision Is Incomplete.

I am guessing when picked up this book you did so because you wanted a better life. I am also willing to bet that you had a vision of what that "better life" looked like. My hope is that as you worked through this book, your vision changed, that you were able to come to a clearer understanding of what you want for your life (and gain the hope that it is possible for you to have that life). Regardless of how much work you have put in this far in the process, you are not done. The vision you now have of your life is incomplete (just as when you started). No matter what your plan is right now, you have no idea the opportunities and challenges that are waiting tomorrow. When I was 18 years old, I never dreamed I would end up being a full time minister. I was going to be a computer scientist. By 30 I was going to be driving a Range Rover, living in a beautiful row house in some major city, married to a beautiful wife. Moving from computer science to ministry was not something that happened overnight. It was a slow process. First, I started helping with a homeless minist at my university. I also started attending a weekly prayer group that challenged 10w the service I was doing, fit into what I believed. The next thing I knew, I was running the homeless ministry. After lots of prayer, I decided that I wanted to do a few years of service after college before getting a traditional job. After much more prayer and soul searching, I was led to do full time ministry.

There is no way I could have made the jump from computer scientist to full time minister. It was a process. Many times, my vocation was not to answer a question by saying "yes", but instead to ask the question. I asked the question,

"Should I do two years of service after college?" By wrestling with the question, it lead me to a new understanding of myself, which lead to a different question, "Should I do full time ministry?"

You have just begun the process to understand what you vocation is, because the way that vocation articulates itself will change at every stage of your life. In every moment, you get the chance to choose who you want to be, in every action you take. The vision you have of your life is incomplete. This should not be a frustration, but instead a hope. More than likely, your vision of your life is richer than when you started this process. I can assure you there is an even richer vision of your life to be found. As you grow in your vocation (and grow closer to God in the process) even more possibilities will come to light.

The dreams, the vision, are not the goal, chasing that vision is. This is not about how the story ends (with our eyes of faith, we know how it ends). It's about the process of becoming who we were made to be, a life filled with abundant joy. If you have worked through all of the exercises in this book, you are well on your way to living a life with passion. The work you have done this far is just the beginning. The extra tools in this section are just a few more items you can add to your arsenal to insure that you are moving in the right direction. The most important thing you can do is to keep trying to move forward. The plan you have is incomplete because you have no idea the challenges, opportunities, and grace that is lurking around the next corner. Keep your eyes and your heart open. As Sir Winston Churchill said during the beginning stages of World War II "This is not the end. It is not even the beginning of the end. But it is, perhaps, the end of the beginning." The best is yet to come.

PART VI

Living Your Vision

Choices

It is easy to recognize the truth in the phrase "you can't take it with you." But to be honest, we don't even have it (whatever "it" is) right now. We can say we own this or that. Really, we are just in custody of the stuff we have. This "ownership" is only a temporary state. Our sense of ownership is supported by our laws. We agree that once you buy something it is yours, and if I were to steal it, there would be consequences. On a much larger scale, there are agreements that say where one country ends and another begins. All of this can change without our consent. Look at the strife happening all over the world. In conflict, the size and shape of countries can change quickly. What was once "owned" by one, is now "owned" by another. We don't even own our own bodies. We can be injured or imprisoned, without just cause. We would like to hope that there would be mechanisms that protect our rights, but these can fail or be replaced.

The only thing we truly own is our choices. Even if we are imprisoned and our options are taken away, we still have the choice of how we are going to respond. We can choose how to act, what we think, and the disposition we take. Our choice exists first in our heart, mind, and soul. That can't be taken away from us without also taking our lives. Do we choose to act with love, or to hold grudges, or to make ourselves better people? Or, do we commit the ultimate sin against our free will and simply not choose? In my mind, it is much worse to surrender our choice, than to make a choice that in the end we regret. Our free will is the greatest gift we have ever been given, because it is the only thing we can truly own. Our ability to choose is sacred. The stuff we own and the stories we tell are not who we are. We are the choices we make. It is only in the choices we make that we can say who we are and what we believe. And I don't mean just the big choices of job, where we live, and who we marry. Every choice we make. The things we buy. The music we listen to. The way we drive. How we interact with a stranger on the street. Every choice we make is one more instance when we put our imprimatur on our lives, stating what we believe and ultimately who we are.

Timing of Dreams

The book you are holding in your hand is a dream come true to me, even if you are the only person who ever reads it. If you were to shoot me up with truth serum, I am sure I could give you a list of all the things I think are wrong with the book. I could also come up with a list of all the things I would have done differently in creating it. It is natural to want something to be the best, as long as perfectionism doesn't consume us. Even with its flaws, it is a dream come true. I have wanted to write this book for over five years. When I would bring the idea up to people that I was working on this book, I would get a number of different reactions. Most of them amounted to a figurative pat on the head, "Oh that is so nice you are writing book." I understand this because I believe half the people in the country are writing a book, at least in their head. Skepticism that the dyslexic computer scientist was really writing a book, is valid. I could go months without writing a word, reading a single article in research, or looking over the pages of typed notes. Still I was writing this book. I would get a speaking gig on the topic. All my old notes would come out and I would be re-energized about the idea and work for a week or two adding new content, but again it would fall to the background. On my goal list I wrote the title of this book everyday for over a year and did little work. Then one day everything changed.

Brad and I had a performance in the Seattle area on Wednesday and one in Tampa on Friday. Thursday, moving from one show to the next, I was on my first flight of the day, flying to Minneapolis. We reach the altitude where portable electronics could be used. I fired up my computer and for some reason I thought to myself I should work on this book. Instead of going back to my old notes, I opened a fresh document and started coming up with chapter and section titles. I moved them around in order, added items, combined items, and the next thing I knew, we were landing in Minnesota. For the next six or eight days, I was writing every day. I was starting to lose sleep because my mind was thinking about the ideas all the time. Then I moved to writing twice a day and reading for two or three hours a day on the topic, just to see how my ideas matched up with other writing. I didn't want to waste my time recreating the wheel. I wanted to make sure I had something new to say, or at least a new way to present things. Then all of a sudden, I lost my enthusiasm. Not because I didn't believe in what I was doing, but I started to feel failure. Not because I was failing right now, but in some ways I failed because it had taken me four years to get the discipline to work on it. I started to mourn the time I had lost. Just as suddenly as my grieving showed up, it left, without warning. Let me explain.

When I write, I usually do it in a burst of 45 minutes to an hour. Before I write, I have a good idea where I am going in a section. As fast as my little fingers can move, the idea comes pouring out of me. I am completely oblivious to the world around me. Many times this writing will happen in a coffee shop, and I will have headphones on with music playing. The world is the screen in front of me. As I finish an idea, I stop writing, pull my headphones off and grasp for air. It is as if I have been underwater working franticly, and only then can I get oxygen into my lungs. It take me a moment or two to re-acclimate to the room I am in, the people coming and going, the sounds of the cafe. It is often only then do I get a chance to reflect on what I have just written. For some reason once I start an idea, the idea just takes over and I am just along for the ride.

I can remember one evening I was sitting in Kiss Cafe in Baltimore, I just finished a section and letting my eyes re-adjust to the lights in room. As I reflected on what I had just written, I realized there is no way that I would have approached that subject the same way four years ago. The book I wrote is radically different (and I hope much better) than the one I would have written four years ago. As much as I would have liked to believe that I could have written this book four years ago, I couldn't have done it. I have learned so much about my own vocation. I have come to realize in a much fuller way, how my dreams drive my life.

I share this story because I think it is very important to understand that sometimes we are not (or the world is not) ready for our dream. We might only have hints of the dream right now, or we might even have the full picture, but we are not ready for it. Don't be frustrated if you think something is truly your calling but doesn't work out. Life is a very long tale. If it is something your soul truly longs to do, it is not going to let failure stop you. It will call the dream forth again and again. We are a work in progress and always will be. It becomes very liberating when we realize that. There is no finish line, and for that matter, no starting line. This is not a race. It is a journey, not to a destination, but to find out who you are right now, and who you can become.

Manna in the Desert

Note: I am not a theologian. And I know it is a dangerous endeavor to explain theological concepts. I do this with trepidation. Know this is not what someone (or anyone) else would conclude. This is what I have learned from one particular story.

By the time we get to the fifteenth chapter of Exodus, we find the Jewish people in the desert. They have escaped slavery and their pursuers are now fish food. They are in the middle of the desert with nothing to eat. Then, something amazing happens. But because it is so human, it is also completely unremarkable. The Jewish people get really mad at God. They turn to Moses and say (this is a paraphrase), "Back in Egypt we might have been slaves, but at least we had food in our bellies. You have led us out into the desert to starve to death." So Moses turns to God to lodge the complaint of his people. God hears the request and is faithful to his people. Each night, He has quail descend on the camp, and each morning as the dew evaporates it turns into bread. The Jewish people are given strict instruction to only gather what they need. Each person gathers what they can, and then the food is distributed throughout the community. This happened daily for forty years. It is written that some of the people tried to hoard extra bread. When they did, it was wormy and useless in the morning. They could only use their daily need. Regardless, and without fail, quail came at night, and bread was found in the morning.

When I read this story, the first phrase that came to mind, was the line from the Our Father, "Give us this day, our daily bread." When we pray that line we are not asking God to give us everything we need. We are simply asking to give us our daily bread, what we need today. Don't feed us for the rest of our lives. Feed us today, because we believe you are faithful enough that you are going to feed us tomorrow.

As you begin to follow your plan, some of the steps are easy to take; others are going to take years, if not your whole lifetime. I believe with my whole heart that when we chase what our soul longs for, we are going to continue to find a store of energy. At times we are going to use very little energy to take a step forward. Other times is it going to take every ounce of energy we have. Burning every bit of fuel. Leaving nothing. Not even the energy to think what the next step will be. Don't be discouraged in these moments. When we are following our soul, each time we use everything we have, feeling like we are lost in the desert, we too, will find our daily bread. All the energy that you have right now, is the energy to get you to the next step. That is all you need. You only need to move one step closer. Only after you have done that, will you be ready to take the next step.

Moral Relativism

Recently, I was giving a talk in Atlanta. I only had forty five minutes with the group so I needed to keep my thesis simple. I decided that if I did my job well, the audience would leave with the belief that they were called to something and that it was not only possible to obtain that calling, but their life would be filled with joy in the pursuit of that calling. That was a big goal for forty-five minutes, but I figured it would be manageable.

At the end of my talk, I had fifteen minutes to take questions. The first few were nothing out of the ordinary. "What is the first step I can take to start to figure out my calling?" "Would you recommend any books?" "What would you suggest I do for a friend who is in a job that is sucking their life?" "Did you bring anything to juggle?" (Somehow this always comes up, which never ceases to amaze me.) Then I was caught by a question out of the blue. I don't remember what the question was exactly, but this is what they were getting at: "So you are saying that we need to do whatever makes our soul happy? No matter what that is? So I can do anything I want? So basically, you are a moral relativist. If it feels good do it, right?"

Yikes!

The question came out of left field. I am sure I looked like a deer in the headlights. There is no way that I did a good job answering that question that evening, but in the end it was (and is) a very good question.

In the end, the answer is "yes" and "no" or maybe "you missed the whole point". Before you get too fired up about my answer, read the whole thing. After you do that, if you want to fire off a scathing e-mail, go right ahead. I would love to hear what you think. I can be reached at gene@monterastelli.com.

As part of my morning routine, as I am recopying my goal list, I make a list of ten things that I am thankful for. Most mornings "freewill" makes it on to the list. I love choices. I am completely fascinated by choices. More than likely, if we were to hang out, sometime over the course of our conversation I would ask you how you got your first name and about the jewelry you are wearing. In most cases names and jewelry have a story behind them. I was named after my grandfather. I got this ring on my first visit to Rome. There was a choice made. Many times the clothing we put on in the morning we simply do out of habit or based on what is cleanest. (I did not say clean, but cleanest. I am a boy after all.) When we only make the choice once, such as naming a child, we give it a lot more thought.

It is so amazing that we have been created with free will. God loves us so much, He wanted to give us the power to create and choose. He could have created us to simply worship Him. Only doing what He wanted us to do. But that is not what He chose to do. We have free will. So to answer the question, we can do whatever we want. We really can. BUT (and it is a big but) that is not the full story.

There are two things to consider. First, in the way the question was phrased, it implied that we could make any choice we wanted without consequence. That is simply not the case. We can choose to charge thousands of dollars to a credit card to buy all sorts of things. It would feel great, but the consequence of that action will be debt that we will have to deal with. We can choose to assault a stranger on the street. In the end, we will have to face the authorities and our Maker. There is nothing from stopping us from making the choice, but simply making the choice is not the end of the story.

The second incorrect implication of the question is that "if it feels good" equates to what the soul longs for. This is also not the case. The joy our soul longs for is at a very deep level. This is not the same thing as happiness in the moment. When we make the choice to follow what our soul longs for there are times in which we are going to sacrifice what we want in the moment. My long term goal may be to lose weight. My short term desire is to eat a piece of cheesecake. These two actions are in conflict. What do I desire more? Obviously, long term health. By choosing the cheesecake, I would be doing what feels good, but not what feels right.

Finally, I think it is important to understand one more belief that I have. I firmly believe that there is nothing that the soul longs for (our deepest calling of who we are) that is contradictory to God's love and God's plan for creation. The same cannot be said for the choices we might make in the moment that feel "good" for the moment. As we have seen, the hard part is trying to figure out what that vocation of our soul is. No matter what our individual calling is, in my heart of hearts, I believe there is no way that this call could be outside the recognition of the fact that we are One Body that cannot be separated. Our calling intimately is in harmony with serving and being in communion with that same Body of Christ.

We can make any choice we want. We have unlimited free will. Just because it might bring us temporary happiness, doesn't mean it is what our soul longs for. Every choice we make is ours. We get to reap it fruits, but also are responsible for all of the consequences. We should not fear our free will, or surrender it to someone else. The most human thing we can do is exercise our will. It is only in these choices can we be in communion with the Body of Christ.

What I Leaned

When I set out to write this book I had a very clear goal in mind. I wanted to write a book that would help those, who love the work they do, find a little balance in their financial lives. Little did I know the journey I was in for. In the beginning, I forced myself to write everyday. Within three days of that my writing schedule was up to twice a day (morning and evening) and I added an hour or two of reading on the topics of money, calling, and work. I thought as the time passed, the book would get harder and harder to write. I figured the initial enthusiasm would pass. That was not the case. There were many times when it was an hour later and I realized I had just learned something new about money, vocation, and myself. Now there were a number of writing sessions where I wrote a bunch of junk. In the end, those moments were gifts because I realized how I didn't want to express an idea.

In trying to articulate what I thought about how money fits into life and vocation, I had to come to terms with a number of core beliefs of my own, which needed to be challenged. In thinking about the theoretical, I had to shine light on my own life and the choices I was making. My hope is not that you put into practice (or for that matter even agree with) the thoughts in this book. My true hope is that you will take time out of your life to try and understand what your hopes and desires are. To look at the core beliefs and fears preventing you from reaching these dreams, and to have the courage to shape a life full of joy. You will never reach your original vision, but you will end up in wonderful places you never dreamed of, constantly growing closer to the person your soul longs to be. Know that with this book, you have taken one more step along your journey. If there is ever anything I can do to help you to continue to refine or execute your dreams, don't hesitate to contact me.

I love chasing dreams, but I also love dreams and dreamers. I love hearing people talk with passion about the life they want, or to hear the stories of the lessons learned from chasing a dream (regardless of whether the dream was realized). One of the reasons I read FORBES magazine is because it is a collections of dreams. I may not be able to relate to the desire to make the greatest copper pipe joint in the world, but I can relate to wanting to solve a problem and to the lessons learned from trying. I know in my life, it has made it much easier to chase my dreams when I am surrounded by dreamers. Sitting next to a dreamer somehow makes my dreams seem more possible. I would be blessed and honored if you would like to share your dreams with me. Just drop me a note. It will give me the courage and strength to keep chasing mine.

I believe it was Buckaroo Bonze who said, "Wherever you are, that is where you are." Once you know where you are, it is up to you to get where you want to be. My prayer is that wherever that is, that you be filled with the challenges and joy of that journey. Stay in touch. Keep dreaming!

¡Que dios te bendiga!

Gene Monterastelli
gene@monterastelli.com

INCOMPLETE READING LIST

- What Should I Do with My Life?: The True Story of People Who Answered the Ultimate Question *Po Bronson*
- Art & Fear: Observations on the Perils (and Rewards) of Artmaking *David Bayles, Ted Orland*
- The Wealthy Barber *David Chilton*
- The Alchemist: A Fable about Following Your Dream *Paulo Coelho*
- The Fifth Mountain *Paulo Coelho*
- New Rules of Money: 88 Strategies for Financial Success Today *Ric Edelman*
- Whistle While You Work: Heeding Your Life's Calling *Richard J. Leider, David Shapiro*
- Callings: Finding and Following an Authentic Life *Gregg Michael Levoy*
- Die Broke: A Radical, Four-Part Financial Plan *Stephen M. Pollan, Mark Levine*
- Second Acts: Creating the Life You Really Want, Building the Career You Truly Desire *Stephen M. Pollan, Mark Levine*
- The Total Money Makeover: A Proven Plan for Financial Fitness *Dave Ramsey*
- Marvin K. Mooney Will You Please Go Now! *Dr. Seuss*
- Eat That Frog!: 21 Great Ways to Stop Procrastinating and Get More Done in Less Time *Brian Tracy*
- The Soul of Money: Transforming Your Relationship with Money and Life *Lynne Twist, With Teresa Barker*
- Unstuck: A Tool for Yourself, Your Team, and Your World *Keith Yamashita, Sandra Spataro*

GENE MONTERASTELLI

Gene was born and raised in Casper, Wyoming. The rumors that he was raised by a pack of wolves are highly overstated. (It was only two, not a pack.) Gene would consider his birth as the most significant moment in his life. "I could not imagine what my life would have been like if I would have never been born." His earliest memories are of playing with Tonka Trucks and drinking cologne. (We think it explains a lot). When he grows up (if it ever happens, our bet is it won't) he would like to be a teacher. As a small child, Gene acquired a taste for Cinnamon Life, which is his favorite food to this day. Gene was a nerd (and some would contest he still is) and loved being on the Math team (from time to time he still likes to wear his pocket protector).

Since 1996, Gene has been 52% of APeX Ministries (APEXMINISTRIES.COM). He out weighs his business partner. As a performance ministry, APeX combines death defying juggling, sketch comedy, drama, and personal testimony. Gene can get out of a straight jacket, pick off little green army men with a bullwhip, ride a unicycle, ride a mini bike, juggle five balls, eat fire, and do a handful of card tricks (not all at once). Gene is on the road over 200 days a year between performing, speaking, and just wandering around. The only place Gene would rather be than on the road, is on the back of a horse.

When he is not on the road Gene visits his few worldly possessions (mostly second hand furniture and the printer for his computer) which can presently be found in Baltimore, MD (for now). One day, Gene hopes to compete as a solo synchronized swimmer in the Olympics.

Gene's reflections on the world can be found a couple times a week at MONTERASTELLI.COM.

Gene would love to hear your questions, comments and feed back. He can be e-mailed at GENE@MONTERASTELLI.COM

SPECIAL THANKS

This book could not have been finished without the help of two people. Thanks to Nora Bradbury-Haehl. Every time she touched the manuscript it got better. I would also like to thank Pete Morelewicz for his work on the design of the book and for putting up with me saying, "I don't like it, but I still don't know what I want." Additional editing was provided by Monica Bradbury-Lareau, Anne Gallagher, Evan David Goodberry, Liz Falk, Elaine Monterastelli, Alma Richards, Kristen Witte, and Joia Farmer, for which I am greatful.

I would like to thank Gene, Rox, Greer, Laney, Brad, and Joia for walking with me daily. Each living in a way that challenges me.

Countless friends and family have shaped how I understand dreams and passion through the lives they live. By modeling what it looks like to chase passion they have shaped this book, but more importantly, my life. It would be foolish to try and name them all. The list would be pages long and still incomplete. For that reason I am not going to try. Even if you are not thanked in a public fashion, know you are in my thoughts and prayers.

SANTA MARIA DEL MEXICANO

A portion of the proceeds from this book go to support the work at Santa Maria del Mexicano. Santa Maria del Mexicano is a school located in Colón, Mexico, a two and half hour's drive north of Mexico City. The school is over 29 years old and it provides education for material poor and orphaned elementary and junior high-aged boys and girls.

For more information about the work done at Santa Maria del Mexicano and how you can support its wonderful work, please visit SANTAMARIAFOUNDATION.ORG

Brother Blue Publishing runs a number of pilgrimages and mission trips each year, including trips to Santa Maria del Mexicano. Information about these trips can be found at BROTHERBLUEPUBLISHING.COM/TRIPS.

OTHER PRODUCTS BY BROTHER BLUE AUTHORS AND ARTISTS

BOOK: Songs of Hope by Jerry Goebel

Jerry has spent years ministering in jails, on the street, with gangs, and with the dying. In SONGS OF HOPE, Jerry reflects on a number of the Psalms through the eyes of this service. Each reflection will challenge you to understand your connection to others in a radical way.

CD: gohomegirl by Joia Farmer

GOHOMEGIRL is Joia's first studio album. Her soulful voice combines Blues and R&B colored with a healthy dose of Rock. The album is a combination of original work and praise and worship favorites. Listen to tracks at JOIAFARMER.COM

AUDIO SERIES: How to Save the World and Retire by Gene Monterastelli

In this six CD series, Gene shares more practical way to live a life with passion without going broke.

BOOK: Everything You Should Have Learned in College, but Didn't by Gene Monterastelli (October 2005)

In Gene's second book from Brother Blue, he provides a transitional guild that every college student needs. In plain English, he covers all the topics that aren't part of the regular college curriculum. This book helps you to create a plan for moving from college into the real world. The book covers everything from finding a job, getting housing, how to fill out tax forms, and the ins and outs of health insurance, all while creating balance in life.

For special discounted prices for purchasing this book, please visit BROTHERBLUEPUBLISHING.COM/SWR01 for details.

IF

If you can keep you head when all about you
  Are losing theirs and blaming it on you;
If you can trust yourself when all men doubt you,
  But make allowance for their doubting too;
If you can wait and not be tired of waiting,
  Or, be lied about, don't deal in lies,
Or, being hated, don't give way to hating,
  And you don't look too good, nor talk to wise;

If you can dream-and not make dreams your master;
  If you can think—and not make thoughts your aim;
If you can meet triumph and disaster
  And treat those two impostors just the same;
If you can bare to hear the truth you have spoken
  Twisted by knaves to make a trap for fools,
Or watch the things you gave your life to broken
  And stoop and build'em up with worn-out tools;

If you can make heap of all your winnings
  And risk it on one turn of pitch-and-toss,
And lose, and start again at your beginnings
  And never breathe a word about your loss;
If you can force you heart and never and sinew
  To serve you long after they are gone,
And so hold on when there is nothing in you
  Except the will which says to them: "Hold on!"

If you can talk with crowds and keep your virtue,
  Or walk with Kings—nor lose the common touch;
If neither foes not loving friends can hurt you;
  If all men count with you, but none too much;
If you can fill the unforgiving minute
  With sixty seconds' worth of distance run—
Yours is the Earth and everything that's in it,
  And—which is more—you'll be a Man, my son!
—Rudyard Kipling

Avoiding danger is no safer in the long run than outright exposure. Life
is either a daring adventure or nothing. —Helen Keller